ADVANCE PRAISE

THE COMMON LAYPERSON most certainly has a modicum of curiosity about the Federal Plea Bargaining process and procedures. The questions might begin with: "What exactly is a plea bargain; what does it mean for someone to plead out?" "What percent of the cases actually go to trial versus those that are plea bargained?" On the other hand, an attorney, new to the process, would want to have sufficient awareness to understand what kind of agreements can actually be made, and in the process of negotiating for a client, what effect each kind has on sentencing exposure.

The book allows a well-read person to discover how over time plea bargaining was recognized as the dominant convention of American criminal procedure. In fact, most criminal trials in federal court are resolved by plea bargains. A study of the history of plea-bargaining would reveal the revolution in tort law brought on a flood of complex civil cases, which ultimately drove judges to a far more efficient settlement of criminal cases, allowing many such cases to now be resolved out of court. The author also provides an honest discussion of the nature, types and goals of plea-bargaining, and offers a variety of styles and strategies not often taught. Words like analysis, negotiation process, plea policies, standards and rules are the foundation of DeGirolamo's extensive work.

The author lives his career with a deep passion for seeing everyone has the opportunity for the best possible legal representation. That passion is more than evident in the pages of *Plea For Mercy: The Anatomy Of The Federal Plea*. They are filled with the opportunity not only for laypersons to gain a deeper awareness, but attorneys on both sides of the aisle to recognize effective plea bargaining as both an art and a science. The book is a comprehensive, up-to-date guideline on the subject; teaching those in the profession to negotiate the best deal for their clients.

~ TR Stearns
Editor, Retired Educator and Superintendent of Schools

PLEA FOR MERCY

THE ANATOMY OF A FEDERAL PLEA AGREEMENT

PLEA FOR MERCY

THE ANATOMY OF A FEDERAL PLEA AGREEMENT

John G. DeGirolamo, Esq.

Ordering Information:

Quantity sales. Special discounts are available on quantity purchases by corporations, associations, and others. For details, contact the publisher at the address above.

Orders by U.S. trade bookstores and wholesalers. Please contact Publisher:

1101 E. Cumberland Avenue, Suite 301-B
Tampa, FL 33602

Printed in the United States of America

First Edition

10 9 8 7 6 5 4 3 2 1

DEDICATION

This book is dedicated to the ones who taught me that hard
work was the rule, not the exception:

Professor James E. Harf, Ph.D.,

John and Joanne DeGirolamo,

and

Gus Widmann,

to name a few.

TABLE OF CONTENTS

Advance Praise   i

Dedication   vii

Table of Contents   viii

Foreword   xv

Acknowledgements   xvii

Introduction   xix

———•———

PART 1

General Law Of Plea Agreements   5

CHAPTER 1   7

    Rule 11   7

    Sample Plea Colloquy From a Magistrate Judge   8

    SECTION 1   24

      Types of Plea Agreements Allowed Under Rules   24

    SECTION 2   25

      Ability to Withdraw from Plea   25

    SECTION 3   26

    Use of Statements Made in Failed Plea Discussions and in a Proffer Session   26

CHAPTER 2   33

    SECTION 1   33

      A Brief History of Federal Sentencing   33

SECTION 2   39

   Current State of the Law   39

SECTION 3   46

   How Does it all Work?   46

SECTION 4   51

   Use of Relevant Conduct under Guidelines   51

SECTION 5   53

   Use of Acquitted Conduct under Guidelines   53

—— • ——

PART 2   **55**

Specific Types of Plea Agreements   **57**

CHAPTER 1   **59**

   Charge Bargaining   59

SECTION 1   61

   Effect of Plea on Maximum Sentence Available 61

SECTION 2   62

   Selecting the Appropriate Guideline Section   62

SECTION 3   63

   Determining the Guideline Range   63

SECTION 4   64

   Determining the Criminal History Category   64

CHAPTER 2   **69**

   Recommendation Bargaining   69

SECTION 1   70

   Pre-Indictment   70

SECTION 2   71

   Using a Waiver of Rights as a Bargaining Chip 71

SECTION 3   72

    Minimum/Mandatory Sentences   72

SECTION 4   75

    Court is not Bound by any Agreement   75

SECTION 5   76

    Effect of Recommendation Below the Guideline Range
                                                         76

CHAPTER 3   **79**

    Stipulation Bargaining   79

SECTION 1   79

    Rules and guidelines   79

    Sentence agreements under Rule 11(c)(1)(C) 80

SECTION 2   81

    Court Must Reject Inaccurate Stipulations 81

SECTION 3   82

    Stipulations That Hurt the Defendant May be Relied
Upon   82

CHAPTER 4   **83**

    Plea Agreements Involving Cooperation   83

SECTION 1   84

    Don't Be Late Be the First to Cooperate 84

SECTION 2   86

    Subject Matter of Cooperation   86

SECTION 3   87

    Undercover Work   87

SECTION 4   88

    Use of Information Against Defendant   88

SECTION 5   90

    Types of Promises Made by the Government 90

SECTION 6   93

  Timing of Sentencing Proceedings   93

SECTION 7   94

  Determination of Breach of Agreement   94

SECTION 8   96

  Penalties for Breach by Defendant   96

SECTION 9   98

  Remedies for Breach by Government   98

SECTION 10   99

  Agreements Regarding Deportation   99

———— • ————

PART 3   **101**

Penalties, The Consequences of Errors, and Party
Acceptance   103

CHAPTER 1   **105**

  Penalties   105

SECTION 1   106

  Common Errors in Penalty Terms   106

SECTION 2   107

  Effect of Errors in Penalty Terms   107

SECTION 3   109

  Factual Basis   109

CHAPTER 2   **111**

  Warnings   111

SECTION 1   111

  Perjury and Other False Statement Offenses   111

SECTION 2   112

  Reinstitution of Prosecution   112

SECTION 3   113

Disclosure of Information to Probation Office and Court   113

SECTION 4   114

Effect on Forfeiture and Civil Proceedings   114

CHAPTER 3   **117**

Collateral Consequences of Plea   117

SECTION 1   118

Loss of Right to Carry Firearms   118

SECTION 2   118

Immigration Consequences   118

SECTION 3   119

Loss of Federal Benefits   119

SECTION 4   120

Military Service and Benefits   120

SECTION 5   120

Federal Contract Exclusion   120

SECTION 6   121

Federal Employment and Licensure/Security Restrictions   121

SECTION 7   121

International Travel   121

CHAPTER 4   **123**

Approval and Acceptance of the Plea   123

SECTION 1   123

Defense Attorney Approval   123

SECTION 2   125

Government Approval   125

SECTION 3   126

Court Acceptance   126

PART 4   **129**

Waivers   **131**

CHAPTER 1   **133**

    Waiver of Trial and Other Constitutional Rights   133

  SECTION 1   133

    Appeal Waivers Must be Knowing and Voluntary   133

  SECTION 2   135

    Waiver of Trial Rights   135

  SECTION 3   136

    Waiver of Right to Appeal the Sentence   136

CHAPTER 2   **137**

    Some Appeal Waivers May be Invalid   137

  SECTION 1   137

    Waiver of Collateral Review   137

  SECTION 2   139

    Waiver of Bradey Material Pre-Plea   139

  SECTION 3   140

    Jurisdictional Challenges Not Waived   140

  SECTION 4   141

    Entirety Clause   141

CHAPTER 3   **143**

    Sample Full Plea From the Department of Justice
Website   143

Author Bio   **161**

Thank you!   **162**

FOREWORD

WHEN I BEGAN my career as a criminal defense lawyer, federal practice was considered elite and obscure. Unless you had served as a federal prosecutor or public defender, the subliminal word was "Stay Away!" I didn't heed these warnings and shoved my way through the thicket of federal procedure and culture. Fortunately, things evened out. But there were more than a few scary adventures on route.

If only I had possessed a copy of John DeGirolamo's excellent "Plea For Mercy!" This valuable work would have made the ride much less treacherous and painful.

Mr. DeGirolamo, a successful and dedicated federal criminal lawyer, does the unusual in this necessary book. Rather than protect and covet his unique knowledge of these problems, obstacles and dilemmas, he shares it. This outstanding young lawyer presents a brilliant, clear and practical explanation of a federal plea bargain so that any interested practitioner can approach the subject with confidence. He does a great service to our profession.

In simple cadence, Mr. DeGirolamo walks the reader through myriad types of federal plea bargains, the common mistakes lawyers make and the unsettling morass of Federal Sentencing Guidelines. He explains the math of how plea bargains either fail or evade their original purpose. And, most importantly, he tells us what to do if things explode!

This work will benefit anyone who practices criminal law. Prosecutors will see the world from another vantage point. Experienced federal criminal defense attorneys will gain clarity and wisdom. And, if, like the younger me, your main experience has been in state court, this book will propel you into the federal system with confidence and insight.

The Federal Courts are great places to practice law. Thank you, John DeGirolamo, for your excellent work.

~ Thomas A. Mesereau, Jr., Esq.
http://mesereaulaw.com/

ACKNOWLEDGEMENTS

IN ACOMPLISHING THIS feat, the author expresses his gratitude to those who judged his book by its cover, fore he will never lack motivation.

INTRODUCTION

I HAVE ALWAYS considered myself a sheepdog. There is a popular analogy, made even more famous by the movie, *American Sniper*. It was originally written into existence by Lieutenant Colonel David Grossman, in his book, *On Combat*, published in 2004. The following is an excerpt from the book:

> *If you have no capacity for violence then you are a healthy productive citizen: a sheep. If you have a capacity for violence and no empathy for your fellow citizens, then you have defined an aggressive sociopath—a wolf. But what if you have a capacity for violence, and a deep love for your fellow citizens? Then you are a sheepdog, a warrior, someone who is walking the hero's path.*

This is how it the analogy was acted out in *American Sniper*:

A small family is sitting around the dining table, sharing a meal. We see the father, the mother, and two young boys. The father decides the time is ripe to dispense some paternal wisdom after one his boys got into a physical confrontation with another boy.

"There are three types of people in this world: sheep, wolves, and sheepdogs. Some people prefer to believe that evil doesn't exist in the world, and if it ever darkened their doorstep, they would not know how to protect themselves. Those are sheep."

He continues:

"Then you've got predators, who use violence to prey on the weak. They're the wolves."

He pauses and looks at his boys:

"And then there are those blessed with the gift of aggression, and an overpowering need to protect the flock. These men are a rare breed, they live to confront the wolf. They are the sheepdogs."

I am a rare breed. I am aggressive. I protect the flock. And I confront the wolf, which, in the world of federal criminal defense, is possibly the mightiest human force on earth, the United States Government.

The truth is, at times, men make mistakes. We don't live in a perfect world. At times, people are wrongly accused or the people that are rightly accused are sentenced unfairly. In your hands is a sneak peak behind the curtain that most people don't even want to admit is there:

Ambition has seductive powers that even the most noble of us can give in to.

People who climb the ranks in any profession are tainted with it, but that is not a bad thing. I, too, am very ambitious.

My name is John DeGirolamo and I'm a Federal Criminal Defense Attorney. I was born in a town called Jenkintown, Pennsylvania with a rare heart defect, Ebstein's anomaly of the Tricuspid valve, which means my tricuspid valves remained flaccid and my blood was free to speed around my heart as if it were in the Daytona 500. Now, obviously I don't remember any of that. It wasn't until years after that I found out about my heart defect and what it meant. The disease remains so rare that doctors to this day give me this, 'No shit' type look whenever I warn them of the pre-existing condition—well, the ones that even know what it is.

Any who, so my life began... in the negative column. I was down points before the game even started. When I think about it, being born behind the proverbial Eight Ball is exactly what shaped the person I am today. Before I even knew how to think, my body learned how to fight.

I've always rooted for the underdog. I'm always the David to the Goliath's of the world, taking on the larger foe from a seemingly weaker position. I'm a fighter, I'm aggressive, I'm not one to back down, and I'm definitely not passive.

There is nothing more satisfying for me than taking on the improbable and coming away with the win.

These qualities are innate and inherent. I didn't learn them from anyone; rather, from the very moment I was born I was being shaped this way.

There wasn't a day in my life that I remember ever wanting to be something other than a criminal defense attorney. There was just something bad-ass about each one I came across. They had this moxie, a glow, if you will. Seemingly, anyone that was a criminal defense attorney looked the part—an obnoxious suit tailored to fit like a glove, a nicely patterned shirt, a tie with a fat knot (what I later discovered to be a *Windsor Knot*), a big fancy car that costs as much as a small house, slicked back hair, a gold watch you could see for miles... they just looked like they had it all. They looked flat-out rich and you know what, they were, every single one of them. God, was that appealing to me. Perhaps to you, that may not seem important and that's okay. I just want you to get a sense of who I am because I have many things to share that I think you will find very important.

Today, as a Federal criminal defense attorney, I have my own practice in Tampa, Florida. I have the fancy car, a pretty girlfriend, and a dog and a cat; I play golf, and have many cherished acquaintances. Becoming an attorney was no easy feat. While I partied like most kids in college, I was ready for it to end. It was just a stepping-stone of sorts before I could get to law school.

A little more about me:

After graduating from the University of Tampa, I attended Barry University School of Law, located in Orlando, Florida. Although I still did my share of partying, I mostly studied alone. When exam time came, I was in shut down mode. No more drinking, no more partying, no more late night excursions; it was every man for himself.

I was never a superstitious person. Nor am I the type to get nervous before big events, such as hearings, trials or exams when I was in college. I like something that Philadelphia Eagles Head Coach Chip Kelly said when he was the Head Football Coach at the University of Oregon, "Nervousness is the feeling you get when you're not prepared." So, on exam days, much like trial days, I was cool, calm, and collected. I always have been.

I remember one day when I was taking the Contracts exam, someone was freaking out. I didn't know much about the guy and didn't remember him speaking much in class, but on that day he was loudly drawing attention to himself by frantically pacing about, asking how much time before the exam started and moving from seat to seat.

"What's his problem?" I asked a friend sitting next to me.

Keeping his voice low he told me, "He keeps saying he forgot to bring his lucky hat."

I scoffed, "Lucky hat? How fucking lucky could it be? We're at Barry…"

Now to the important stuff…

I love being an attorney. I have the car, the girl, the gold watch and everything else I wanted… everything except the slick back hair that is, proof of the universe's unfairness as my grandfather on my mother's side gave my genes a bit of the bald. Either way, I have zero regrets on the path I've chosen. It has brought me to where I am today, successful and writing this book.

There are a ton of attorneys in the world but by comparison, there are very few trial lawyers. I've been taught by and have gone up against some of the best, and there is a stark difference between an attorney and a trial lawyer. I'm a trial lawyer. My practice concentrates on defending individuals and corporations who have been accused of a federal crime by the United States. Clients that have been arrested at the state level do retain me, but for the most part, my practice is geared towards defending those who have been summoned one way or the other, involuntarily of course, by the Department of Justice wing of the United States government.

In June of 2014, I was nominated and selected to join the National Trial Lawyers of America. I was also selected as a Top 40 trial lawyer under 40 years of age in Florida.

According to the acceptance letter, "Membership into the Top 40 Under 40 is by invitation only and is extended exclusively to those individuals who exemplify superior qualifications, trial results, and leadership as a trial lawyer."

It was and is a great honor. It's always flattering to be recognized for what you do, and being recognized for being an exceptional trial lawyer is like hitting a grand slam with two outs, three balls and two strikes, in the bottom of the ninth inning to win the World Series. However, just because I'm an accomplished trial attorney, it does not mean every case I get hired on goes to trial. The fact that is, a really good trial attorney knows when to take a case to trial and when not to. The reality is: most criminal cases at the federal level are resolved by plea bargains because it is in the best interest of the defendant, the client.

Now you...

If you are an attorney who is still searching for tailored suits, the gold watch, fancy car, Windsor Knotted ties, and everything else I mentioned, you might want to consider becoming a federal criminal defense attorney. If you are considering becoming a federal criminal defense attorney, I wrote this for you!

This book is intentionally designed to take you through the ins and outs of a criminal plea from start to finish, including pre-indictment negotiations, post-indictment bargaining, cooperation tactics, and the ever so confusing *Federal Sentencing Guidelines*. You will know everything you need to know to make the decision on whether or not you have what it takes.

I look out for those that need help.
I fight the United States government on
behalf of my clients.

Maybe you can too...like the sheepdog *you* were born to be.

This may be where this book gets boring for some, and takes off for others. I encourage you to keep reading (I can safely assume you have not put me down already). I told you earlier that I would tell you what this book was about once I told you a little bit about me. The balance of the book will take you through the ins and outs of a federal criminal plea, from start to finish, including pre-indictment negotiations, post-indictment bargaining, cooperation, and a discussion of the ever so confusing *Federal Sentencing Guidelines*. Just because I'm a trial lawyer does not mean every case I'm hired on goes to trial. I would even take that a step further and argue that part of being a trial attorney is knowing when *not to go to trial*. In reality, most criminal cases at the federal level are resolved by plea bargains because it is in the best interest of the defendant, your client.

Federal criminal defense lawyers are trained in a way that they can offer the best defense to a defendant. The most competent federal practitioners have the ability to figure out arguments that go in the favor of the client that state court practitioners won't know, and they have the ability to give arguments that can negate a crime altogether. Further, federal criminal defense lawyers are well versed in the rules and regulations, and can play a vital role in creating awareness and knowledge about these rules. Federal criminal defense lawyers work with the defendant and the prosecutor to strike the most favorable deal for the defendant. These deals are plea bargains.

Most people, lawyers and defendants alike, are not aware of the hidden, true value of participating in the plea bargain process. A plea bargain can help reduce the sentence or eliminate some of the charges that have been brought in an indictment. In order to negotiate a successful plea agreement, federal defense counsel must understand what kind of agreements can be made and the effect of each kind on the client's sentencing exposure. Plea bargains are generally referred to and treated as agreements, and they are akin to contracts in a heavily regulated industry. Rights and responsibilities under these contracts are controlled by a multitude of statutes, rules, guidelines, policies, and of course, case law. Regardless of the type of plea agreement, defense counsel must understand the impact of all these layers of regulation in order to know what the provisions of the agreement will mean to the client.

The Department of Justice requires that plea agreements for all felonies (and misdemeanors negotiated down from an original felony charge) be reduced to writing and filed with the court. Some U.S. Attorney's offices have standard plea agreement forms, while others give more leeway in what can or must be in the plea agreement. Indeed, some agreements cover just the basics in a few succinct pages, and others extend to ten and sometimes twenty pages, which would be my preference so that nothing is missed and everything that has been a part of the plea negotiations is covered. Ensuring both parties are protected.

This book sets out the basic federal rules, discusses the *Federal Sentencing Guidelines*, typical policies, and provides analysis of plea agreements in federal criminal court. Throughout many of the Chapters, I provide typical provisions that show up in many standard federal plea agreements for purposes of analysis and comprehension. At the conclusion you will find a complete and comprehensive example of a federal plea. En-joy.

PLEA FOR MERCY

THE ANATOMY OF THE FEDERAL PLEA

PART 1

GENERAL LAW OF PLEA AGREEMENTS

*Unless you have a perception of who you are as a
lawyer, you will never be at ease in dealing with legal
matters, clients, or courts.
But if you know who you are and why you're there, all you
need is the expertise and the information.*

~ Samuel Dash, Esq. (1925 – 2004)
American professor of law and chief counsel for the
Senate Watergate Committee

General Law Of Plea Agreements

A DEFENDANT WHO is considering a plea is usually primarily concerned about what he or she will plead guilty to and what penalties will be assessed. Although the shape of the plea is controlled by many fact-specific factors related to the crime and the defendant, there are some general principles of law and policy that impact on:

> the prosecutor's initial charging decision,
>
> the amount of prosecutorial discretion available for bargaining,
>
> the involvement of the court in the bargaining process, and
>
> the defendant's ability to enforce the plea bargain once it is entered.

These general matters are the primary subjects of this Section. Specific ramifications of the various kinds of plea bargains available in federal court are covered in Part 2.

Plea bargains are controlled or influenced by various sources of law. Federal court practitioners are familiar with Rule 11 of the Federal Rules of Criminal Procedure (FRCrP), which, together with case law interpretations, sets out much of the basic law on plea bargaining. Certain portions of the *Federal Sentencing Guidelines* (USSG or Guidelines), in particular §1B1.2-4 on Relevant Conduct and §6B1 on Plea Agreements, also have a strong effect on plea bargains. Probably the least familiar source of information is the Department of Justice (DOJ) Manual, which should be available in local court libraries and in local federal defender offices.

CHAPTER 1

RULE 11

———— • ————

FEDERAL RULES OF Criminal Procedure Rule 11, FRCrP, sets out the basic ground rules for all plea bargaining in federal court. Much of the case law regarding how the plea hearing is handled and the effects of various pleas is based on interpretation and analysis of Rule 11. It should be the first source consulted on any plea question. The following are some notable provisions of the rules. Citations to the rules in this Section are to the FRCrP unless otherwise stated.

Types of pleas allowed under rules:

Rule 11(a) describes the kinds of pleas allowed under the Federal Rules as "not guilty," "guilty," and "nolo contendre" (better known as "no contest"). From a practical standpoint, in federal criminal law, there is no such thing as a "no contest" plea because the defendant accepts responsibility as part of his or her voluntary plea and thereby accepts and admits guilt. That said, under certain circumstances a defendant may enter a nolo contendre, conditional plea under Rule 11(a)(2) with the consent of the court and the government in order to preserve an issue for appeal. If the defendant prevails, he may withdraw the plea upon remand.

SAMPLE PLEA COLLOQUY FROM A MAGISTRATE JUDGE

When a defendant chooses to plea, he or she will do so at a "change of plea hearing." Because he or she previously plead not guilty, and now wishes to plea alternatively, there is a change of plea. Outlined below is a very thorough sample of the questions a judge will go through with all parties involved when accepting the defendant's plea at a change of plea hearing.

Judge To Counsel:

"I understand that your client wishes to plead guilty to Count(s) _____ of the Indictment [pursuant to a Plea Agreement] [without a Plea Agreement], is that correct?"

Judge To the Defendant:

"I am not the Judge who will sentence you if you plead guilty. I am a Magistrate Judge. I can conduct a guilty plea proceeding with your permission. I have a document signed by you indicating that you agree to let me do that. Is that correct?"

"I am going to have you placed under oath and ask you some questions. The first group of questions is designed to make sure you understand what the proceeding is about— and then I talk to you about what the United States would have to prove as to each count to which you propose to plead guilty. We will talk about the penalties you face and the rights that you lose if you plead guilty. [I will also review the promises in the plea agreement.] At the end, I'm going to ask you what you did to make sure your conduct violates the crime(s) to which you propose to plead guilty."

"Because you will be under oath, if anything you tell me is not completely truthful, you could then be separately prosecuted for perjury or making a false statement and anything you tell me today could be used against you in that prosecution. So, if you do not understand something I ask, please let me know and I'll try to ask the question more clearly. Your lawyer will be here throughout the proceeding and you may speak with him privately at any time. We make a record of what occurs here through a digital recording, which is the reason for the microphones. So I need to you answer my questions out loud rather than nodding or shaking your head."

"Do you have any questions before I proceed further?"

Judge to the Courtroom Deputy Clerk:

"Please place the defendant under oath."

Courtroom Deputy Clerk to the Defendant:

"Do you solemnly swear or affirm that the testimony you shall give in the cause before this Court will be the truth, the whole truth and nothing but the truth? Please state your name and spell your last name for the record."

Judge to the Defendant:

"Have you ever been known by any other name?"

"How old are you?"

"How far did you go in school?"

"Do you read, speak and understand English? If not, are you able to understand what I am asking as it is being translated for you?"

"Are you a citizen of the United States?"

"The next group of questions is designed to make sure you understand what this proceeding is about."

"Have you ever been under the care of a psychiatrist or psychologist?"

"Are you currently taking medicine of any kind?"

"If so, what is the name of the medicine or what is it for?"

"In the last two days, have you taken any drugs, alcohol or medicine, other than any prescription medicine, including anything over-the-counter like aspirin? If you are taking prescription medicine, is the medicine, or lack of prescribed medicine, or the underlying condition for which the medicine has been prescribed making it difficult for you to think clearly today?"

"Is there anything that is interfering with your ability to think clearly and concentrate today?"

"Next, I will review the charges to which you propose to plead guilty and tell you what the United States would have to prove before you could be found guilty."

The judge will then read or summarize each count of the indictment to which the defendant proposes to plead guilty and tell the defendant the essential elements that will have to be proved for each count.

<u>Judge to the Defendant</u>

"Do you understand what would have to be proved before you could be found guilty of the charge in Count(s) ___?"

"You have the right to have the full indictment read to you. I have only read parts of the indictment. Would you like to have the full indictment read to you or do you waive or give up the reading of the full indictment because you have already reviewed it with counsel?"

"Have you reviewed the indictment with your attorney?"

"Have you had enough time to speak with your attorney?"

"Are you satisfied with your attorney's representation of you in this case?"

<u>Judge to Counsel:</u>

"Do you have any questions about your client's competency?"

"Does the United States have any question about the defendant's competency?"

<u>Judge to the Defendant:</u>

"I find that you are competent, which means that you are able, under the law, to plead guilty if you want to plead guilty, but you do not have to plead guilty. I have a number of things I need to discuss with you, so if at any time in this proceeding you decide you do not want to plead guilty, please let me know. I will stop this proceeding and the case will continue as previously scheduled."

"Next, I need to speak with you about the reason you are proposing to plead guilty."

"First, has anyone done anything wrong or unfair, or threatened you in any way to get you to plead guilty to this charge(s)?"

"Do you want to plead guilty because you committed the crime(s) or for some other reason?"

If no plea agreement the Judge will add the following question:

"Has anyone made any promises to you regarding the sentence you will receive or anything else that will occur in exchange for your guilty plea(s)?"

With a plea agreement the Judge will add the following questions:

"I have a document entitled plea agreement. I am going to ask my courtroom deputy clerk to hand it to you. I want to make sure it is your plea agreement and that you have initialed every page and every change and signed it at the end."

"Is that your plea agreement?"

<u>Judge to Counsel for the United States:</u>

"Is that the plea agreement of the United States?"

<u>Judge to the Defendant:</u>

"None of the Judges of the Court helped to write this plea agreement. It will be up to the judge who will sentence you if you plead guilty, to decide whether or not to accept the terms of the plea agreement."

"Did you read the entire plea agreement before you signed it?"

"Did you speak with your lawyer about the plea agreement before you signed it?"

"Do you believe that you understand the plea agreement?"

"I am not going to read the whole document. I am going to go over the promises you make to the United States and the promises the United States makes to you. When I am finished, I am going to ask you if you believe there are any other promises that are not contained in the plea agreement."

The Court then reviews the promises in the plea agreement

If property is subject to forfeiture:

"The plea agreement provides that you will forfeit or give up to the United States money or property gained during the commission of the offense or used during the offense. Under the Constitution of the United States, all of us are protected from having an excessive fine imposed. An argument could be made that requiring you to forfeit money or property as part of the punishment you receive in this case violates the excessive fine clause. Under the plea agreement, you agree that you will not make that constitutional argument."

"Have you spoken with your attorney about that constitutional right?"

"Is that a right that you are willing to give up?"

"The plea agreement also discusses your right to appeal from or challenge a mistake in your sentence. I want to review that with you. First, let me tell you that if you plead guilty, you are admitting for all time that you committed this crime(s). You give up any defenses or excuses you may have, you also give up any motions your attorney has filed or you've spoken with him about filing, and you give up the right to come back to this court or go to another court and argue that you should not have been found guilty. The right to come back to this court or go to another court is called the right to appeal. So, if you plead guilty, you have no right to appeal from the finding that you are guilty."

"If you think the judge makes a mistake in the sentence you receive, you usually do have the right to ask for that mistake to be corrected. You can do that by filing a direct appeal to the next higher court or by collaterally challenging your sentence, usually by filing a paper in this court under 28 U.S.C. § 2255. Under the plea agreement, you are giving up some of your rights to appeal from or collaterally challenge a mistake in your sentence. You can only do that if the sentence is above the sentencing guideline range as is determined by the court, if the sentence is more than the sentence permitted by the law, or if the sentence violates the Eighth Amendment to the Constitution, which is your protection against cruel and unusual punishment. However, if the United States appeals from your sentence, then you have the right to file a direct appeal for any reason."

"Do you understand how that limits your right to appeal from or collaterally challenge a mistake in your sentence?"

"Is that a right you are willing to give up?"

[Following review of the plea agreement promises]

"Those are all of the promises written in the plea agreement. Has anyone made you any other promises about what sentence you will receive or anything else that will occur in exchange for your plea of guilty?"

"Next, I will review the maximum possible penalties you face if you plead guilty to the charge(s). (The court will advise the defendant of the maximum and minimum mandatory penalties) The judge who will sentence you will look at something called the Sentencing Guidelines to help decide what sentence you should receive in this case. The judge must consider the Sentencing Guidelines, but he or she is not required to impose a sentence within the sentencing guideline range."

"Have you and your attorney discussed how the sentencing guidelines might apply in your case?"

"I cannot tell you what your sentencing guideline range will be for you because I do not have all of the information I need. If you plead guilty, the court's probation office will conduct a presentence investigation. They will look at what happened, and whether you accepted responsibility or if you have any prior criminal history, and things of that nature in order to prepare a written report. You and your attorney will receive a copy of the report before the sentencing. The attorney for the United States will also receive a copy of the report. Your lawyer can make an objection if there is anything in the report that you think is not correct. If the objection is not resolved before the sentencing, then the judge who will sentence you will hold a hearing and rule on the objection. Only at the point that the report is finished and the judge has ruled on the objections will there be enough information to know your sentencing guideline range."

"Your lawyer is giving you his best estimate of what the sentencing guideline range is likely to be, but he can't know for sure until the presentence report is prepared and the objections are ruled on. So, it is important for you to understand that if the sentencing guideline range or the sentence is something different than you expect it to be, then you would not be allowed to withdraw your guilty plea for that reason."

"If you happen to learn what the sentencing guideline range is for someone else who committed a crime similar to the crime(s) you propose to plead guilty to, you should not assume that you can calculate your sentencing guideline range based on the range for another person. That is because the sentencing guideline range is an individualized determination. So, for example, if two people committed the very same crime, but one of them had more criminal convictions than the other, the person with the greater number of criminal convictions is almost always going to have a higher sentencing guideline range than the person who has fewer or no prior criminal convictions. Also, some people may qualify for departures from the sentencing guideline range as there are many individual factors the sentencing Judge considers."

"That's a long explanation because it is important that you understand that if the sentencing guideline range or the sentence turns out to be something different that you expect it to be, you cannot withdraw your guilty plea for that reason. Is that clear?"

"We do not have parole in federal prison system anymore. That used to be a form of early release. Now, if you are sentenced to a term in jail, you will serve almost all, if not all, of any term of imprisonment imposed."

"I mentioned supervised release as part of a possible sentence. Supervised release is a time a defendant serves under the supervision of the Court's probation office after getting out of jail. Probation is a time served by a defendant under the supervision of the court's probation office without going to jail in the first instance. There will be things that you must do, and things that you cannot do, under either type of supervision."

"If you violate a condition of supervision, then your supervision can be taken away. You could be sent to jail if you violate probation. In the case of supervised released, you could be sent back to jail to serve the term of supervised release in addition to the time you served on the original sentence. If you are not a citizen of the United States, then you may be deported or removed from the United States as a result of being convicted in this case. If you are deported or removed before you complete your term of supervision and you later come back to the United States—legally or illegally —you will still be required to finish your term of supervision. In other words, your supervision does not go away simply because you are deported or removed from the United States."

"You could be required to contribute financially to the cost of your supervision if you have the money to do so."

In controlled substances cases:

"You should know that in drug cases such as this one, you may be required to forfeit certain benefits from the federal government for a period of time. Those benefits include the right to vote, the right to serve on a federal jury, the right to hold federal office or employment, and the right to enlist in any services of the armed forces or receive payment of any veteran benefits. There could also be occupational restrictions if your crime has a reasonable direct relationship with your occupation. If you have a federal or professional license you could lose that as a result of your crime."

"You could be disqualified from any type of service related to a labor organization or employee benefits plan and you could be made ineligible for grants, licenses, contracts, and other federal benefits, excluding retirement, welfare, Social Security, health, disability and public housing. You are also not eligible to receive food stamps or temporary assistance to needy families, and the amount payable to any family or household of which you are a member is reduced proportionately [21 U.S.C.§§ 862a(a)]"

In child pornography and other sexual offense cases:

"After you complete your term of imprisonment, an evaluation will be conducted to determine whether it is safe to release you from custody. If there is a concern about whether you can be released, you may be subject to additional civil commitment after your criminal sentence is completed. You may also be required to register under the Sex Offender Registration and Notification Act. If you change your state of residence, then you will need to notify the Federal Bureau of Investigate and the new state of residence of your move. Failure to comply with those registration requirements is a separate felony offense."

"You will be required to cooperate in the collection of a DNA sample if the law requires a sample."

Judge to Counsel for the United States:

"Are there any other penalties applicable to the defendant that I overlooked?"

Judge to Defendant:

"Do you understand all the possible penalties you face if you plead guilty to this charge(s)?"

"Next, I am going to review with you the rights you lose if you plead guilty."

"You have the right to a trial before a jury composed of 12 people. During the trial you would be presumed to be innocent. The United States would have to prove that you were guilty beyond a reasonable doubt. You wouldn't have to prove anything."

"During the trial, the witnesses would have to come into Court and testify in front of you. Your lawyer could ask them questions, and he could ask the Judge to keep out all or parts of anything the witnesses said and all or parts of any other evidence offered against you."

"You would also have the right to require witnesses and evidence to be brought into court and presented to the jury on your behalf. During the trial, you could testify—talk to the jury under oath—if you wanted to, but you also have the right to not testify and neither the Judge nor the jury could decide that you did anything wrong based on your decision not to testify. That is your right against self-incrimination and it gives you the absolute right to remain silent.

"If you plead guilty and the District Judge accepts your plea, do you understand that there will be no trial, you give up any defenses or excuses you have and all the rights I've talked about, including the right to remain silent, and the District Judge will find you guilty based on your guilty plea?"

If no plea agreement:

If you plead guilty, you are admitting for all time that you committed the crime(s). You give up any defenses or excuses you may have and all motions your attorney filed for you or you talked about filing, and you give up the right to come back to this court or go to another court and argue that you should not have been found guilty."

"The right to come back to this court or go to another court is called the right to appeal. So if you plead guilty, you have no right to appeal from the finding that you are guilty. If you think the judge makes a mistake in the sentence you receive, you can appeal from the sentence but not from the finding that you committed the crime."

"Do you understand that difference?"

"The crime(s) to which you propose to plead guilty is a felony offense. If you plead guilty, you will lose your civil rights. Those include, but are not limited to, the right to vote, to keep and bear firearms, to hold public office and to serve on a jury. There is a right you do not give up by pleading guilty, and that is the right to be represented by an attorney."

"If you decide to go to trial, your attorney will represent you at trial and at every other stage of the case. If you decide to plead guilty, your attorney will represent you all the way through the sentencing. If you believe the judge makes a mistake in the sentence you receive and you want to appeal from the sentence, subject to the limits in the plea agreement that we talked about, the court would appoint an attorney to represent you for the direct appeal if you could not afford to hire someone."

"I've talked about many things. Do you have any questions about anything I've talked about?"

"Do you have any questions about anything in the plea agreement that I did not talk about?"

"What did you do that makes you guilty of the crime charged in Count(s) ____?" (The defendant will be required to admit in his own words what he did that establishes each element of each offense to which the defendant wishes to plead guilty.)

Judge to Counsel for the United States:

"Counsel for the United States now provides the factual basis from the United States."

Judge to the Defendant:

"Is what the United States says it could prove true to the extent it talks about what you did and what you knew?"

"I find that the facts are sufficient to allow you to plead guilty if you still want to do that. I told you when we started that you did not have to plead guilty. Now we are getting close to the time when I am going to ask you how you would like to plead."

"First, though, is there anything you want to tell me or ask me that bears on your decision to plead guilty that we have not talked about?"

"Would you like to change anything you told me under oath that you think might not have been completely truthful?"

"Have you had any problems hearing or understanding anything during the proceeding?"

"Do you want to speak with your attorney further before I ask you how you would like to plead?"

Judge to the Counsel for the United States:

"Are there any victims who wish to be heard?"

Judge to the Defendant:

"How then do you plead to the charge in Count(s) _____ of the Indictment?"

"Are you freely and voluntarily entering this plea(s) of guilty?"

"I find that the plea(s) of guilty is knowingly, intelligently and voluntarily made. It is not the result of force or threats or promises [other than the promises contained in the plea agreement.] I will recommend that the District Judge accept your guilty plea [and the plea agreement.]"

"Sentencing is usually at least 75 days from today because that is how long it takes to do the presentence investigation. I do not have the sentencing date for you. Your attorney will tell you when sentencing is scheduled and he will also explain the presentence process to you."

———— • ————

SECTION 1

TYPES OF PLEA AGREEMENTS ALLOWED UNDER RULES

———— • ————

Rule 11(c)(1) describes the kinds of pleas allowed under the FRCrP and provides that the government can:

(A) agree not to bring, or to dismiss, other charges in return for a plea,

(B) make a recommendation to the court, or agree not to oppose a defendant's recommendation, that a particular sentence or range is appropriate or that a particular guideline provision/policy/factor does or does not apply (non-binding), and

(C) agree that a sentence or range is appropriate or that a particular guideline provision/policy/factor does or does not apply (binding once plea accepted).

———— • ————

SECTION 2

ABILITY TO WITHDRAW FROM PLEA

————— • —————

Rule 11(c)(4-5) combine to allow the defendant to withdraw from the plea if a plea under 11(c)(1)(A) or 11(c)(1)(C) is rejected by the court. In essence, this is a back to square one provision. Unfortunately, if the plea agreement includes a requirement that the defendant perform some action prior to the sentencing, such as participating as a confidential source, it is difficult to get all the way back to square one. If a recommendation under 11(c)(1)(B) is rejected, the defendant cannot withdraw under this rule.

In general, Rule 11(c)(1) forbids the court to participate in any plea bargaining discussion. For example, case law dictates that a meeting between the judge, prosecutor, defendant, and defense counsel in chambers, off-the-record, during which the judge stated openly that he agreed with the prosecution's recommendation about 90% of the time, is unacceptable under Rule 11(c)(1). Similarly, the Court crossed the line into the realm of forbidden participation in plea bargaining where defendant got cold feet at the change of plea hearing after the judge told him (1) that if he was tried on all three counts he would have to get 15 years, (2) that if he pled guilty he would get 10 years, and (3) that he should talk to his lawyer to see if that is really what he wanted to do.

SECTION 3

USE OF STATEMENTS MADE IN FAILED PLEA DISCUSSIONS AND IN A PROFFER SESSION

———— • ————

Rule 11(f) relies on Rule 410 of the Federal Rules of Evidence (FRE), to determine the admissibility of pleas, plea discussions, or related statements. Thus, ordinarily, counsel need not worry about the use of such statements against the client except in the two situations specifically excepted by Rule 410: First, an exception providing a rule of completeness that allows the rest of a statement to be admissible at trial where part of it has already been admitted, and second, an exception for use in perjury prosecutions.

To my chagrin, the Supreme Court has held that the protection of these rules is presumptively waivable. The Supreme Court permitted proffer statements made in plea discussions to be used as prior inconsistent statements in cross-examination at trial and to be proved up by a law enforcement agent who attended the proffer meeting. The basis for that holding came from the typical proffer letter signed by the defendant, which contains language that is wholly consistent with using an inconsistent statement at trial against the defendant.

A proffer is an exchange of information between you, the suspect and law enforcement. The defendant can generally admit to criminal activity, and in exchange they will be immunized from culpability linked to any admissions. Proffer sessions are usually used for white collar crime investigations and rarely used for "street crimes." The people at the proffer session will be you, your attorney, one or more Assistant U.S. Attorneys, as well as members of law enforcement agencies involved in your case such as the FBI, ATF, IRS Criminal Division, Department of Homeland Security, etc.

The meeting takes place in a conference room, not a courtroom, and it is rather informal. More importantly, there is no court reporter or audio recording so you are left with no one, unless your attorney will become a witness, to support your version of events. However, federal law enforcement usually has the highest professionalism and integrity so you rarely have to worry about someone "coloring" your statement.

Prior to the proffer, the defendant's attorney will obtain a letter immunizing the defendant. A proffer letter sets forth the understanding pursuant to which a witness or defendant provides information to the government in anticipation of formalizing a cooperation agreement. Generally, it provides only use immunity, which I will further discuss below. The letter does not, however, protect the witness against the derivative use of the information, also discussed below.

There are two standard immunities. First, there is "proffer letter immunity" or "use immunity," which is the weakest immunity provided by the government. Normally, the government won't grant the defense a more significant kind of immunity without knowing a lot about what information the defendant can provide. This immunity allows the defendant to participate in the proffer knowing what he or she says won't be used against him or her in a future criminal proceeding. However, this is not absolute and carries with it two exceptions. First, the government can use what the defendant says to collect evidence to use against him. For example, a defendant could state "I killed Tom Smith with a shotgun and the shotgun is in my basement." In this scenario, the government cannot use the admission that he killed Tom Smith against him, but they can go to his basement, obtain fingerprints from the shotgun, match the ballistics from the shotgun to the bullet found in Tom Smith, and prosecute him using that evidence without the statement.

The second exception is if the defendant makes a different or conflicting statement under oath at a later time, the government can use the earlier proffer statement and compare it to the conflicting statement against the defendant in a later proceeding, whether that be to discredit testimony provided by the defendant, or in a case against the defendant.

The government generally insists on limiting proffer letter immunity to use immunity. This protects the government in the event of a failure to reach a cooperation agreement. Should the government later decide to prosecute the witness where only use immunity was conferred, the government will not be required to prove an independent source for all subsequently acquired information.

"Derivative use immunity" is the second commonly used immunity in proffers. This immunity protects a witness against the direct and indirect use of the information provided by the witness. After a grant of derivative immunity, the government may not use statements and/or admissions, either the actual words or information provided, nor any information or evidence derived as a consequence of the statements. This is a very strong immunity, but again is rarely offered to a defendant.

Personally, I think the defendant would be more forthright under this type of immunity. Since defendants are typically reluctant to participate in a proffer session, derivative immunity eliminates, with some exceptions, the trust issues a defendant has with the government. It is a very difficult and an often-awkward situation for a defendant to sit across from the same person(s) who will likely in the future try to send him or her to prison.

Prior to any proffer session with the government, the client should be told in the most forceful terms that the government would consider "almost truthful" information to be worthless. It is either l00% truthful or it is useless. Many government proffer letters advise that should the prospective witness be untruthful at any point during the proffer, the immunity offered for the proffer is deemed withdrawn and the information provided can be used against the defendant.

For obvious reasons, a client should be fully debriefed by his or her defense attorney prior to the proffer so that the defendant is fully aware of what may be asked and what is expected. Far too often, a defendant thinks that he or she does not have to provide truthful and complete information and may try to protect a family member or close friend and "rat" on everyone else. Further, the client may believe that he or she is only required to be truthful concerning information about the crime itself. The client must know, prior to meeting with the government, that there are no "safe harbors" of information.

Moreover, the government may decide that the defendant is being truthful, but the quality and/or quantity of the information provided during the proffer session or cooperation is marginal at best, or is of no value to the government. In this circumstance, even though the defendant has been operating in good faith, the government can seek to make derivative use of the information provided by the defendant, which provides a great advantage to the government in conducting any subsequent investigation of the client, but is the exact reason why a defendant is hesitant to be completely forthright. There is no guarantee that the government won't absorb the defendant's information, decide the information is just not good enough, and either (a) have that information used against him or her, or (b) grant little to no reduction in his or her sentence. The same goes if the defendant begins cooperating, but later refuses to complete the cooperation to the extent originally contemplated and agreed to by the parties. This event would be a clear breach of the proffer or cooperation agreement and would be the figurative equivalent of the defendant shooting him or herself in the foot.

If the client has information that is of value to the government and is honest and forthcoming with the government, then it can be reasonably assumed that there will be no problems during the course of the defendant's proffer and future cooperation. I always tell my clients before a proffer, "The government knows the answers to half the questions they are asking you and they are merely testing you to see if you tell the truth when they ask those questions.

If you lie, and they know it, they will continue with the proffer knowing you already lied to them because you have now waived your immunity and evidentiary protections under the proffer letter. In other words, you may think you are outsmarting them, but in truth, they have you right where they want you."

When the defense finds itself in a situation where the proffer and cooperation discussions break down or fail, or where the defendant is caught being untruthful, which can all happen for any number of reasons, protecting the defendant against future harm becomes the top priority of defense counsel.

———— • ————

CHAPTER 2

FEDERAL SENTENCING GUIDELINES

—•—

The *Federal Sentencing Guidelines* impact plea bargaining in several ways and have added a new dimension to the analysis of the benefits and pitfalls of any plea bargain. Counsel can now see with some reasonable clarity the effect on the sentence that a particular bargain or agreement might have on the defendant. The guidelines are also set up on their own standard for when judges should accept or reject plea bargains.

SECTION 1

A BRIEF HISTORY OF FEDERAL SENTENCING

—•—

FORGIVE ME, I really did not want to do this at any point in this book, but I'm going to get pretty lawyer-ish right here. It's an important context for this Chapter and the book for that matter. I'll do my best to clean it up.

A long while back, federal judges had the authority to impose sentences as they saw fit in criminal cases. Certain judges were known for light sentencing and others were known for harsh sentencing. Congress decided that this was a problem in the early 1980's. They felt that federal sentencing should be predictable across the board; for example, a defendant sentenced for a federal crime in Michigan by Judge Jones should receive roughly the same sentence as a defendant sentenced for the same crime in Florida by Judge Smith. The word being thrown around was "disparity."

Effective November 1, 1987, Congress created a system known as the United States Sentencing Guidelines, which reduced federal sentencing to a formula based on tiered calculations. Every federal crime was assigned a certain number of points called a "base offense level." The level was increased by "specific offense characteristics," such as the dollar amount of loss in a white-collar fraud case or the total quantity of cocaine in a drug distribution case. The Guidelines further adjusted the offense level for issues such as the use of a weapon, obstruction of justice and acceptance of responsibility. Adding and subtracting the various points yielded the "adjusted offense level."

A separate point total was then determined for the person's record of prior convictions to determine the "criminal history points" of the defendant. The more prior convictions meant more points. Those points were then compared against the sentencing table, specifically the top of the table, to conclude the defendant's "criminal history category."

Finally, the adjusted offense level and the criminal history points were taken together to determine a sentencing range from a graph, with the adjusted offense level on the vertical side of the graph and the criminal history points on the horizontal. The intersection of the two points on the graph was a sentencing range that gave the judge a minimum number of months and a maximum number of months. A range of 70-87 months, for example, meant that the judge was required to impose a sentence of at least 70 months but not more than 87 months. In theory, the judge was not allowed to go above or below the Guideline range, absent rare findings of "upward departures" or "downward departures," which are sentences above or below the Guideline range, respectively.

———— • ————

John G. DeGirolamo, Esq.

SENTENCING TABLE
(in months of imprisonment)

Zone	Offense Level	Criminal History Category (Criminal History Points)					
		I (0 or 1)	II (2 or 3)	III (4, 5, 6)	IV (7, 8, 9)	V (10, 11, 12)	VI (13 or more)
Zone A	1	0-6	0-6	0-6	0-6	0-6	0-6
	2	0-6	0-6	0-6	0-6	0-6	1-7
	3	0-6	0-6	0-6	0-6	2-8	3-9
	4	0-6	0-6	0-6	2-8	4-10	6-12
	5	0-6	0-6	1-7	4-10	6-12	9-15
	6	0-6	1-7	2-8	6-12	9-15	12-18
	7	0-6	2-8	4-10	8-14	12-18	15-21
	8	0-6	4-10	6-12	10-16	15-21	18-24
Zone B	9	4-10	6-12	8-14	12-18	18-24	21-27
	10	6-12	8-14	10-16	15-21	21-27	24-30
	11	8-14	10-16	12-18	18-24	24-30	27-33
Zone C	12	10-16	12-18	15-21	21-27	27-33	30-37
	13	12-18	15-21	18-24	24-30	30-37	33-41
Zone D	14	15-21	18-24	21-27	27-33	33-41	37-46
	15	18-24	21-27	24-30	30-37	37-46	41-51
	16	21-27	24-30	27-33	33-41	41-51	46-57
	17	24-30	27-33	30-37	37-46	46-57	51-63
	18	27-33	30-37	33-41	41-51	51-63	57-71
	19	30-37	33-41	37-46	46-57	57-71	63-78
	20	33-41	37-46	41-51	51-63	63-78	70-87
	21	37-46	41-51	46-57	57-71	70-87	77-96
	22	41-51	46-57	51-63	63-78	77-96	84-105
	23	46-57	51-63	57-71	70-87	84-105	92-115
	24	51-63	57-71	63-78	77-96	92-115	100-125
	25	57-71	63-78	70-87	84-105	100-125	110-137
	26	63-78	70-87	78-97	92-115	110-137	120-150
	27	70-87	78-97	87-108	100-125	120-150	130-162
	28	78-97	87-108	97-121	110-137	130-162	140-175
	29	87-108	97-121	108-135	121-151	140-175	151-188
	30	97-121	108-135	121-151	135-168	151-188	168-210
	31	108-135	121-151	135-168	151-188	168-210	188-235
	32	121-151	135-168	151-188	168-210	188-235	210-262
	33	135-168	151-188	168-210	188-235	210-262	235-293
	34	151-188	168-210	188-235	210-262	235-293	262-327
	35	168-210	188-235	210-262	235-293	262-327	292-365
	36	188-235	210-262	235-293	262-327	292-365	324-405
	37	210-262	235-293	262-327	292-365	324-405	360-life
	38	235-293	262-327	292-365	324-405	360-life	360-life
	39	262-327	292-365	324-405	360-life	360-life	360-life
	40	292-365	324-405	360-life	360-life	360-life	360-life
	41	324-405	360-life	360-life	360-life	360-life	360-life
	42	360-life	360-life	360-life	360-life	360-life	360-life
	43	life	life	life	life	life	life

November 1, 2013

With the Sentencing Reform Act's creation of the United States Sentencing Commission and the subsequent promulgation of the Sentencing Guidelines, Congress sought to provide certainty and fairness in meeting the purposes of sentencing. 28 U.S.C. 0 991(b)(l)(B). In contrast to the prior sentencing system, which was characterized by largely unregulated discretion, and by seemingly severe sentences that were often sharply reduced by parole, the Sentencing Reform Act and the Sentencing Guidelines sought to accomplish several important objectives:

(1) to ensure honesty and transparency in federal sentencing;

(2) to guide sentencing discretion, so as to narrow the disparity between sentences for similar offenses committed by similar offenders; and

(3) to provide for the imposition of appropriately different punishments for offenses of differing severity.

As a general rule, the Guideline penalties were harsh. The judge at sentencing made the findings of fact required by the Guidelines as a "preponderance of the evidence" standard. Preponderance of the evidence is a burden of proof used in the American Justice system and is commonly defined as "just enough evidence" to make it more likely than not that the present claim or assertion is true. That was a low burden at sentencing compared to the high burden at trial of beyond and to the exclusion of every reasonable doubt. Taken in conjunction with minimum/mandatory sentences set by statute for specific crimes such as drug offenses, the Guidelines encouraged many people to plead guilty. This was especially true because one of the most effective ways to get a "downward departure" from the Guideline range was to cooperate with the Government by providing information about co-defendants or others committing crimes. The Guidelines effectively transformed federal criminal defense into the business of encouraging your client to plead guilty and cooperate as soon as possible, so as to maximize the chance that his information would be useful to the Government in prosecuting someone else. If your client didn't, his co-defendant would, and your client would be taking the brunt of the points for the criminal acts under the Guidelines.

The guidelines were not without their flaws. One of the potential constitutional issues with the Guidelines was the violation of a defendant's right to a jury trial. If we all have a Sixth Amendment right to be tried by a jury, then why did the judge have the power to increase the person's sentence based on facts found at sentencing without a jury? The question became more urgent in federal court after the Supreme Court issued landmark decisions applying to state court cases in *Appendix v. New Jersey*, 530 U.S. 466 (2000), and *Blakely v. Washington,* 542 U.S. 296 (2004). The decisions held that a judge could not go beyond the jury's factual findings and impose an aggravated sentence based on additional facts found by the judge at sentencing. Federal practitioners wondered if the same rule could be applied in federal court. The answer was a resounding "maybe."

In *United States v. Booker*, 543 U.S. 220 (2005), the Court held that the federal Guidelines violated the Sixth Amendment right to trial by jury. This is the single most important sentencing guideline case established to date. Specifically, the Court found that at sentencing, when the judge made the findings required by the Guidelines, he or she was going beyond the facts found by the jury at trial (or admitted by the defendant as part of his plea). The defendant could not be sentenced with a mandatory system of Guidelines that required these additional findings of fact at sentencing. So we know the problem, but what was the solution? *Booker* made the Guidelines "advisory," rather than mandatory. The judge would continue to do all of the Guideline calculations, but the Guideline sentencing range would no longer bind the judge. Instead, it would be one factor among many for the judge to consider at sentencing. As long as the judge was not *required* to impose a sentence within the Guideline range, the Court found no Sixth Amendment problem in directing the judge to *consider* the Guideline sentence as a non-binding recommendation.

SECTION 2

CURRENT STATE OF THE LAW

For those of us in the trenches, the new system comes with the same old challenges. Although *Booker* requires that the sentencing court consider myriad sentencing factors in addition to the U.S. Sentencing Guidelines, the fact remains that the overwhelming majority of sentences are within the applicable guideline range. Less than 10 percent of cases involve what we call "*Booker* variances," which involve sentences below the guideline range based on consideration of the statutory factors set forth in 18 U.S.C. § 3553(a), discussed below. It is an understatement to say that many of us federal criminal practitioners were pleased by the *Booker* decision. The Guidelines had been put in their place, judges were free to be judges and lawyers finally had an opportunity to do real, dedicated lawyering for their clients at the plea bargaining stage, and of course, at sentencing.

As stated above, the Court post-*Booker* should *consider* the guideline range calculation as merely one of many factors under § 3553(a). The overriding principle and basic mandate of § 3553(a) requires district courts to impose a sentence "sufficient, but not greater than necessary," to comply with the four purposes of sentencing set forth in Section 3553(a)(2): (a) retribution (to reflect seriousness of the offense, to promote respect for the law and to provide just punishment); (b) deterrence (to dissuade others from participating in or performing the same conduct as the defendant); (c) incapacitation (to protect the public from further crimes); and (d) rehabilitation (to provide the defendant with needed educational or vocational training, medical care, or other correctional treatment in the most effective manner).

In determining the sentence minimally sufficient to comply with Section 3553(a)(2) purposes of sentencing, the court must consider several factors listed in Section 3553(a). These factors are: (1) "the nature and circumstances of the offense and the history and characteristics of the defendant;" (2) "the kinds of sentence available;" (3) the guidelines and policy statements issued by the Sentencing Commission, including the (now non-mandatory) guideline range; (4) the need to avoid unwarranted sentencing disparity; and (5) the need to provide restitution where applicable. 18 U.S.C. § 3553(a)(1), (a)(3), (a)(5)-(7).

Early decisions looked promising. Cases such as *United States v. Hughes*, 401 F.3d 540 (4th Cir. 2005) held that in light of *Booker*, "the discretion of a sentencing court is no longer bound by the range prescribed by the guidelines." Id. at 546. Over time, however, our enthusiasm began to fade as decisions from the various circuit courts of appeal took an increasingly more restrictive view of *Booker*.

How did this happen? If the only appellate review was for a determination of reasonableness, then what basis did the appellate courts find to reverse and remand below-Guideline sentences? The answer: they held that a sentence within the Guideline range was "presumptively reasonable," and although at times logic went out the window, the inescapable corollary was that a sentence below the Guideline range was presumptively unreasonable, and that was tough to swallow.

The trend was illustrated in three cases published by the Fourth Circuit in the first half of the year 2006. The first involved defendant, Charles Green, who pled guilty to distributing crack. He qualified for an especially harsh sentence under the Guidelines because he was a "career offender," a status reserved for defendants with bad records. Pursuant to a plea agreement, Green pleaded guilty to the conspiracy count. The agreement provided that, given the amount of drugs involved, the base offense level under the Sentencing Guidelines was thirty-four, but because Green qualified under the Guidelines as a career offender, the base offense level would be thirty-seven and the criminal history category would be six. After considering factors such as Mr. Green's young age, his efforts to obtain employment after his previous arrests, and the defendant's lack of any involvement with violence or guns, the trial judge did not sentence Mr. Green as a career offender, leading to a much lower than anticipated sentence. *United States v. Green*, 436 F.3d 449, 453-54 (4th Cir. 2006). Specifically, the trial Court concluded that Green had a total offense level of twenty-seven, as opposed to thirty-seven, resulting in a guideline range of eighty-seven to one hundred and eight months' imprisonment. The Court sentenced defendant Green at the low end of the Guidelines to eighty-seven months' imprisonment. *Id.* Hey now! A win for the bad guys!

Oh wait a minute, spoke to soon - the Fourth Circuit reversed: "Even though it is now a given that the Sentencing Guidelines are advisory, district courts are not left with unguided and unbounded sentencing discretion." *Id.* at 455. The Fourth Circuit said that in refusing to impose a sentence within the Guideline range, the district court "simply expressed disagreement with Congress' decision to base career offender status on two prior drug offenses, without any need to involve firearms or violence." *Id.* at 459. The Fourth Circuit also said that the career offender guideline reflected the policy of Congress and that "[t]he district court was not free to ignore that policy judgment and substitute [its own]."

With all due respect to the Fourth Circuit, if the judiciary is a co-equal branch of government, and if the Supreme Court ruled that the Guidelines were merely advisory, *why* does a court lack the authority to substitute its policy decision for those expressed by Congress in the

42

Guidelines? Perhaps limiting the application of a harsh general policy in a particular case based on specific facts is an essential feature of the checks and balances in our constitutional government.

The second Fourth Circuit case in this trend involved Brian Moreland, a man charged with two counts of possession with intent to distribute crack cocaine. Mr. Moreland went to trial and was convicted. At sentencing, he too was found to be a career offender. Based upon his offense and his prior convictions, the Guideline sentencing range was thirty years to life. But the trial court considered the 3553(a) factors and found that the sentencing range "grossly overstated [Mr. Moreland's] prior criminal conduct." *United States v. Moreland*, 437 F.3d 424, 428 (4th Cir. 2006). As a result, the court imposed a sentence of ten years, the mandatory minimum under the statute.

On appeal, the Fourth Circuit reflected on its role in reviewing post-*Booker* sentences and then vacated the sentence and remanded for resentencing. Our task in reviewing a post-*Booker* federal sentence is to determine whether the sentence is within the statutorily prescribed range and is reasonable. Although this standard clearly requires us to afford a degree of deference to the sentencing decisions of the district court, 'reasonableness' is not a code-word for 'rubber stamp.' "*Id.* at 433 (internal quotation marks omitted).

Having gotten over the rubber stamp hurdle, the Fourth Circuit then uttered the words that effectively reinstated mandatory Guidelines: "[a] sentence that falls within the properly calculated advisory guideline range is entitled to a rebuttable presumption of reasonableness." *Id.* Did you feel the wind just go out of our sails? A Guideline sentence is reasonable; a below-Guideline sentence is not. To be sure, the Fourth Circuit protested that its decision did *not* mean that a below-Guideline sentence was "presumptively unreasonable," but the damage to *Booker* had been done. *Id.* Applying the principles to Mr. Moreland's case, the Fourth Circuit "conclude[d] that the district court committed a clear error of judgment by arriving at a sentence outside the limited range of choice dictated by the facts of the case." *Id.* at 436 (citations and quotes omitted).

The final decision in this ugly trend was *United States v. Johnson*, 445 F.3d 339 (4th Cir. 2006). Artez Johnson pled guilty to three drug counts. His Guideline range was 97-121 months, but his creative lawyer urged the trial court to impose a lower sentence. The lawyer argued that the trial court was not bound by the advisory Guidelines and that the court should refuse to apply the "grouping" provisions of the Guidelines that resulted in a higher sentencing range. The trial court rejected the argument and imposed a sentence within the Guideline range. The Fourth Circuit affirmed. Citing *Green* and *Moreland*, the court declared that "certain principles" were relevant at any sentencing, and "*foremost among these* is that a sentence within the proper advisory Guidelines range is presumptively reasonable." *Id.* at 341 (emphasis added). Why? For several reasons, according to the court.

First, they've done it this way for a long time. "By now, the Guidelines represent approximately two decades of close attention to federal sentencing policy. It would be an oddity, to say the least, if a sentence imposed pursuant to this congressionally sanctioned and periodically superintended process was not presumptively reasonable." *Id.* at 342.

Second, the Guidelines already account for all of those pesky sentencing factors in 18 U.S.C. 3553(a). No need to weigh the other factors along with the Guideline sentencing range, because "[t]he 3553(a) factors are built into the Guidelines." *Id.* at 343. Apparently, this point eluded the Supreme Court in *Booker*, which expressly "require[d] a sentencing court to consider Guideline ranges, but [ ] permit[ted] the court to tailor the sentence in light of other statutory concerns as well, *see* 3553(a)." *Booker* at 757 (citations omitted).

Third, the Guidelines themselves are fair and just to criminal defendants. "[T]he Guidelines range applicable to each defendant is an individualized determination." *Id.* at 343. "To assure reliability, the defendant may object to those facts with which he disagrees, requiring the district court to rule on any disputed portions of the presentence report. The entire process, in short, is designed to lead to a full and credible set of facts particular to the defendant himself." *Id.* at 344.

It may be that to a careful reader, the decision in *Johnson* sounds more like legislative policymaking than judicial reasoning. Perhaps the Fourth Circuit was substituting its policy decisions for those of the Supreme Court? Be that as it may, it is the law of the land in federal court in North Carolina.

So, in a nutshell the current "official" policy to follow at sentencing in federal court is: First, the court determines the Guideline range. Second, the court considers whether a sentence within the Guideline range serves the sentencing factors in 3553(a). If not, the court decides whether any of the narrow Guideline grounds for "downward departure" or "upward departure" should be applied. If even then the court determines that the sentence does not fit with the 3553(a) factors, the court is legally permitted to give a higher or lower sentence based upon those factors.

There are only two types of permissible sentence bargains, which are discussed in greater length later in this book. Federal prosecutors may enter into a plea agreement for a sentence that is within the specified guideline range. For example, when the Sentencing Guidelines range is 18-24 months, a prosecutor may agree to recommend a sentence of 18 or 20 months rather than to argue for a sentence at the top of the range. Similarly, a prosecutor may agree to recommend a downward adjustment for acceptance of responsibility. These issues and more are expanded upon over the course of this book. In all cases, the court must stay within any mandatory minimum or maximum sentence provided by statute for the offense of conviction.

SECTION 3

HOW DOES IT ALL WORK?

———————— • ————————

Taking all of the information presented above, the following is a synopsis of how the guidelines work in practice. The concepts below are meant as a primer for the more expansive discussions throughout the rest of the book.

Whether you plead guilty or are found guilty after a trial, generally you will be sentenced about 10-11 weeks later. In some cases you can be sentenced sooner. As noted, the Guidelines are an advisory set of rules for all federal sentences. Attorneys will review a defendant's Guidelines with him or her, to show how these rules apply to the case and the sentencing. After the guilty plea, in advance of the sentencing, the U.S. Probation Office assists the judge in figuring out what sentence the defendant should receive. After a guilty plea or verdict, a probation officer will want to interview the defendant, called a Presentence Interview, or "PSI."

The probation officer works for the court and is not an advocate like the defendant's lawyer is; however, in practice, one will find that the probation officer is more neutral than one would think. Defendants and their lawyers do not have to speak to the probation officer, but it is recommended that the defendant speak to the probation officer with counsel since they are the liaison between the parties and the Judge. The last thing one wants is for the probation officer to tell the judge the defendant and his or her attorney did not give him or her the time of day or want to discuss any part of the case or Guidelines. Defendants are, of course, advised not to lie to the probation officer. It is a crime to do so and may lead to an even worse sentence. In some instances, upon the advice of an attorney, it is advisable not to answer one or some of the questions; however, rather than an outright refusal, I would recommend having an off-the-record conversation with the probation officer regarding the issue so that everyone remains on the same page.

After the interview, the probation officer will write a Presentence Report for the judge. The "PSR" discusses the defendant's case, background, family, criminal history, education, career, mental and physical health and other information. Probation may interview family members or employers and may check the information provided in the interview. The probation officer may also speak to the prosecutor and case agent. Probation also figures out the expected Guidelines scores and sentencing range and recommends a specific sentence within the Guidelines range to the judge for the defendant. The judge relies heavily on Probation's recommendation.

The probation officer will send a copy of the PSR to the defendant's lawyer. The Defendant and attorney will get to review the PSR and ascertain if there are any factual mistakes. The lawyer will then review the document for legal mistakes. The lawyer may file objections to the PSR about any changes that should be made and provide reasons, case law, or other support for his or her argument. The judge will consider any objections at the sentencing hearing and decide whether to revise your PSR before it becomes final.

The problem facing the defense lawyer is that determination of the guideline range in a particular case is a multi-stage process, with relevant conduct being considered in different ways at different stages. Initially, a specific guideline from Chapter 2 where there is a guideline for each general type of offense is selected to be used as a basis for calculation for the offense of conviction without regard to relevant conduct. USSG §1B1.2(a). This is called the "base offense." Within that chosen guideline, the base offense level, which is the number of points assigned to the base offense for calculation, and the applicability of various specific offense characteristics and cross references are all based on relevant conduct. USSG §1B1.2(b),3(a). Adjustments under Chapter 3 for issues like role in the offense, obstruction of justice, or acceptance of responsibility are also based on relevant conduct and can contribute to the calculations. USSG §1B1.3(a).

The Guidelines work by giving scores to two different parts of the case: (1) the defendant's criminal record, and (2) the particular offense for which he or she will be sentenced. A chart tells the judge what sentence the Guidelines recommend in the case, according to these two scores. First, the Guidelines rate the defendant's criminal history by giving "points" to each of any prior convictions. The total number of "points" will put the defendant in a "Criminal History Category," ranging from I to VI. Figuring out the Criminal History Category can be very complicated. The defendant and his or her attorney will discuss this issue in detail.

Second, the Guidelines rate the actual offense. The Guidelines give a particular score, called an "Offense Level," to every federal offense. The scores range from 1 (for very minor offenses) to 43 (for very serious offenses). This number may then be "adjusted" according to the particular characteristics of the case. Adjustments can raise or lower the Offense Level. For example, if the defendant pleads guilty he or she will usually get points for "acceptance of responsibility" and that will downwardly adjust the Offense Level.

The Guidelines Sentencing Table is a chart that shows what sentence is required for all possible combinations of Criminal History Category and Offense Level. Based on the defendant's Criminal History Category and Offense Level, the Table will give a sentencing "range." This is the number of months that a defendant could spend in prison. The "low end" of the range is the minimum that the Guidelines recommend the judge sentence the defendant and the "high end" is the maximum the Guidelines recommend. For example, if a defendant's "range" is 121- 135, this means that the Guidelines recommend the judge sentence anywhere from 121 to 135 months in prison. Figuring out the Guidelines can be the most difficult and important part of a case. A properly advised defendant will know his or her likely Guidelines range before entering a guilty plea or electing to go to trial. "Departures" from the recommended Guidelines sentencing ranges are allowed in some situations. The judge can depart upward, giving the defendant a sentence higher than the Guidelines range, or downward, giving a sentence lower than the Guidelines range. Departures are rare and are usually reserved for the most heinous of crimes.

———— • • ————

SECTION 4

USE OF RELEVANT CONDUCT UNDER GUIDELINES

---•---

The concept of relevant conduct has its genesis in USSG §1B1.3. A detailed analysis of relevant conduct is too broad a topic to be addressed in this book and could be an entire book or article in that of itself. Nevertheless, more detail about the use of relevant conduct under specific types of plea bargains is given in Section 3. In general, relevant conduct includes all conduct that occurred during the commission of the offense of conviction, but can be looked at with a more detailed eye. For example, under USSG §1B1.3(a)(1)(A), relevant conduct can be conduct occurring during the preparation for or attempt to avoid detection or responsibility for that offense provided that the defendant aided, abetted, counseled, commanded, induced, procured, or willfully caused the conduct. Further, if the offense was a joint criminal activity, conduct is relevant if it was in furtherance of the activity and was reasonably foreseeable. USSG §1B1.3(a)(1)(B).

In a white-collar case, for example, the dollar amount involved in the fraud was a specific offense characteristic. The higher the amount, the longer the sentence. But the jury had no role in determining the amount. The jury found the person guilty beyond a reasonable doubt of the offense charged in the indictment, but the judge determined the amount of loss by a preponderance of the evidence at sentencing. Therefore, the judge, based on evidence presented at *sentencing*, was free to increase the loss amount based upon "relevant conduct," as opposed to only the evidence presented to the jury. I agree with what you are likely thinking – the foregoing process (a) decimates the "right to a trial by a jury of your peers" as provided for in the constitution and (b) trivializes the jury's role in a deciding what actually happened in a particular criminal event.

The rules are different in a multiple defendant case, as defined in USSG §3D1.2(d), and the seriousness of which is usually measured in a quantity like weight of drugs or number of dollars. In those cases relevant conduct also includes conduct that was part of a common scheme or plan with the offense of conviction. USSG §1B1.3(a)(2). Finally, in what is often seen as a "catch all," relevant conduct also includes all harm flowing from any of the above-described conduct, and any special items specifically identified in any applicable guideline. USSG §1B1.3(a)(3-4).

It is fairly reasonable to assume that relevant conduct can and will be considered by the judge in one form or another at sentencing. This can sometimes negate the value of a plea bargain, although the defendant can often derive substantial benefit from the application of a particular guideline based on pleading to a particular charge. The defendant may also benefit from the removal of certain relevant conduct from the sentencing calculus because of the dismissal of some charges, or the particular wording used in the "factual basis" portion of the plea bargain.

SECTION 5

USE OF ACQUITTED CONDUCT UNDER GUIDELINES

———•———

Judicial consideration of acquitted conduct is logically egregious. A jury, at one time, made a positive choice and verified the defendant's guilt at trial. Sentencing, based upon conduct the jury acquitted the defendant of, however, allows a judge to affirmatively disregard the jury's affirmative decision not to verify guilt. Indeed, the structure of the criminal system demands that facts be proved beyond a reasonable doubt. That charge fails when the government cannot meet this exacting standard. Allowing judicial consideration of acquitted conduct based on argument from the government not only permits the government to argue under a dissimilar burden of proof (preponderance of the evidence), but it also disregards the jury's determination that the prosecutor failed to meet his burden at trial (beyond a reasonable doubt). True, an acquittal does not necessarily mean "innocence," but without asking the jury to rule on innocence specifically, then the jury's finding that the government failed to meet the reasonable doubt standard constitutes "legal innocence."

Proponents of judicial consideration of acquitted conduct may advance a different assertion: in order for the defendant to proceed to sentencing, the jury must have convicted him of something, and thus, the jury has specifically authorized some punishment and consideration of acquitted conduct simply allows the judge to select the proper punishment within a broad range. In fact, the circuit courts reviewing the post-*Booker* use of acquitted conduct put forth this exact rationale, holding that so long as a judge sentences the defendant within the applicable guideline range, the sentence is valid and any facts considered to arrive at the sentence are constitutionally acceptable. Nevertheless, this rationale suffers from two flaws: first, it overstates the extent to which the Guidelines are now advisory, and second, it affords illogical weight to the facts and evidence that the jury so clearly rejected at trial.

———•———

PART 2

SPECIFIC TYPES OF PLEA AGREEMENTS

— • —

Resilience is accepting your new reality, even if it's less good than the one you had before.

~ Elizabeth Edwards, Esq. (1949 – 2010)

SPECIFIC TYPES OF PLEA AGREEMENTS

———•———

This Section discusses the three types of plea bargains recognized under the rules of criminal procedure and the sentencing guidelines: charge bargaining, recommendation bargaining, and stipulation bargaining. It also covers some other forms of bargains that are not mentioned in the rules but are prevalent: pre-indictment bargaining, factual stipulations, restitution agreements, cooperation agreements and agreements related to deportation.

Plea-bargaining must honestly reflect the totality and seriousness of the defendant's conduct and any departure must be accomplished through the application of appropriate Sentencing Guideline provisions. Federal criminal law and procedure apply equally throughout the United States. As the sole federal prosecuting entity, the Department of Justice has a unique obligation to ensure that all federal criminal cases are prosecuted according to the same standards. Fundamental fairness requires that all defendants prosecuted in the federal criminal justice system be subject to the same standards and treated in a consistent manner.

CHAPTER 1

CHARGE BARGAINING

———— • ————

Charge bargaining, which is the agreement to dismiss or not charge certain counts, or to substitute a less serious charge for a more serious one, is one of the most effective bargaining tools. Absent extremely unusual circumstances, judges cannot prevent the prosecution from dismissing charges and can never force them to file charges. Agreements to dismiss or not to pursue charges are authorized under Rule 11(c)(1)(A). In the usual case, an agreement not to prosecute a defendant on other criminal charges is binding only in those judicial districts identified in the plea agreement.

In most instances, the specific charge to which the defendant will plead will have little impact on the ultimate sentence because in calculating the advisory guideline level, all relevant conduct is considered, regardless of the specific count of conviction (more on that later). Generally, a prosecutor must pursue the most serious, readily provable charge consistent with the nature and extent of the defendant's criminal conduct.

The court is required to advise the defendant that it may reject the agreements and that the defendant can withdraw if that occurs. Rule 11(c)(3)(A). Further, USSG §6B1.2(a) advises the court to accept such agreements if the court determines for reasons stated on the record, that the remaining charges adequately reflect the seriousness of the actual offense conduct and that accepting the agreement will not undermine the statutory purposes of sentencing or the sentencing guidelines.

Charge agreements may be useful in certain cases. For example, where you represent a noncitizen, the statute of conviction may have a dispositive impact on whether the defendant will be deported. In addition, where the advisory guideline range would result in a significant prison sentence or fine, the count of conviction can serve as a cap that limits the client's exposure. Also, the applicability of statutory mandatory minimum sentences is controlled by the count of conviction rather than relevant conduct. Finally, there may be collateral consequences like debarment or professional disciplinary sanctions that are impacted by the specific count of conviction rather than relevant conduct.

With regard to charge agreements that serve to cap a sentence below the otherwise applicable guideline range, this may be more tempting to prosecutors than they would choose to admit. Particularly in cases involving multiple defendants, prosecutors do not want to fact bargain or guideline bargain in a manner that might come back to haunt them when it comes time for your client to testify against others, assuming there is a cooperation deal, or to seek a substantial sentence for the codefendant or coconspirator who choses to go to trial. Obviously, where other defendants or potential defendants are involved, a prosecutor will want the client to commit to a version of the offense that is consistent with what the prosecutor hopes to prove against the remaining targets or defendants. In addition, the prosecutor will not want to agree to a guideline calculation other defendants could point to later as justifying a more lenient sentence. Where, for example, your client definitely is facing more than five years at the time of sentencing under the advisory guidelines, and where you expect a judge would impose the guideline sentence, one should push for a plea to a statute with a five-year maximum, perhaps 18 U.S.C. § 371. This achieves your goal of limiting your client's sentencing exposure, but permits the prosecutor to set forth all of the incriminating facts he or she hopes to prove against the codefendants and establish the "appropriate" advisory guideline range.

SECTION 1

EFFECT OF PLEA ON MAXIMUM SENTENCE AVAILABLE

Even under the Guidelines, the court is limited to the statutory maximum sentence for the offense or offenses of conviction. In some cases, the consideration of relevant conduct under the Guidelines, along with the application of various upward departures, may drive the guideline range to an unacceptable height. Although it is difficult to control guideline calculations, pleading to an offense with a maximum of five years as opposed to one with a maximum of ten years at least gives the client some protection.

SECTION 2

SELECTING THE APPROPRIATE GUIDELINE SECTION

————— • —————

The guideline sentencing range and the eventual sentence in a particular case are influenced by, among other things:

(a) the selection of the appropriate guideline to serve as the basis for calculating the base offense level,

(b) the decision to apply various adjustments to that guideline based on analysis of the conduct relevant to the offense of conviction,

(c) the determination of the defendant's criminal history category, and

(d) the decision to apply an upward departure. The effect on each of these of a bargain dismissing charges is discussed below.

Although almost all-relevant conduct can be considered in some form at sentencing, USSG §1B1.2 & 3, the selection of the actual guideline Section to be applied is determined by the charge of conviction. USSG §1B1.2(a). The defendant can often derive some benefit from having the choice of guideline, and thus the base-thirteen offense level, based on conviction for a particular charge. Other relevant conduct is then relegated to consideration only in terms of specific offense characteristics or possible departures. Thus a plea agreement can be effective by preventing the use of dismissed counts in deciding which guideline to apply.

The guideline benefit of pleading to a lesser charge can be nullified if the oral or written plea agreement contains a stipulation that specifically establishes a more serious offense. In such cases, the court may apply the guideline appropriate to the more serious conduct. USSG §1B1.2(a) and (c). However, such a stipulation takes effect only if the defendant and government explicitly agree that it is to be used for that purpose. USSG §1B1.2, comment. (n.1). Counsel should also be alert to the possibility of a cross reference to another guideline. For example, the guideline on obstructing or impeding officers, USSG §2A2.4, refers the court to the assault guideline, USSG §2A2.2, if the conduct constituted aggravated assault.

SECTION 3

DETERMINING THE GUIDELINE RANGE

———— • ————

USSG §1B1.3 provides that, once the appropriate guideline Section has been selected based on the offense of conviction, all relevant conduct should be used to determine the applicability of specific offense characteristics, cross-references, and adjustments and thus the actual guideline range under the chosen guideline. Conduct that constitutes or is related to counts that are dismissed or not charged pursuant to a plea bargain can still influence the guideline calculation if that conduct is found to be relevant to the offense of conviction. The definition of relevant conduct is discussed more fully in Chapter 2 | Section 4, but in general it includes: all conduct that the defendant aided, abetted or was otherwise personally responsible for, conduct in a joint criminal activity that was foreseeable and in furtherance of the activity, and conduct in a group-able offense that was part of a common scheme or plan with the offense of conviction. This is a very broad definition, particularly in conspiracy cases. If the level of an offense depends on some quantity such as the weight of drugs or the number of dollars involved in a fraud, such that it would be group-able under §3D1.2, then the quantities involved in the dismissed counts will be considered in determining the guidelines.

SECTION 4

DETERMINING THE CRIMINAL HISTORY CATEGORY

———■·■———

The guidelines assign each offender to one (I) of six (VI) criminal history categories based upon the extent of the defendant's past criminal misconduct. The conduct to be considered is not just prior federal offenses and includes state court offenses. A specific point total is assigned to each applicable past sentence. The more points assigned to the defendant based on his prior record, the higher the Criminal History Category. Ranging on the sentencing guideline table from left to right, Criminal History Category I is the least serious category, and Criminal History Category VI is the most serious category. Discussed below is a list, although not exhaustive, of criminal conduct that does and does not count in the calculation of the Criminal History Category.

A defendant receives:

Three points for each prior sentence of at least thirteen (13) months.

Two (2) points for each prior sentence of at least sixty (60) days.

One (1) point for any other prior sentence, with some exceptions.

Two (2) more points if he committed the current offense while on probation, parole, supervised release, currently imprisoned, participating in a work-release program, or is considered under the guidelines as "escape status."

Two (2) additional points are assessed if the defendant committed the current offense in prison.

Two (2) additional points are assessed if the defendant committed the current offense less than two (2) years after completing a sentence of at least sixty (60) days.

Some sentences are not included in the criminal history calculation because they occurred too long ago. A sentence of more than thirteen (13) months does not count against the defendant if the sentence was *imposed* more than fifteen (15) years before the defendant *began* to commit the current offense. Here, there can be a distinction between the conviction date and date imposition of the sentence, and when the current crime *began*, such as the beginning of a conspiracy, and the date of conviction or the date imposition of the sentence. There is an exception: a sentence imposed more than fifteen (15) years ago counts if the defendant committed the current offence less than fifteen (15) years after he was released from prison on the prior sentence. This analysis is very case and fact specific, but defense attorneys must calculate dates against the criminal history rules down to the hour.

Some minor offenses will never add points to the defendant's criminal history, such as loitering, hitchhiking, or public intoxication. Other sentences will count only if the defendant received at least thirty (30) days in jail or prison, or one (1) year of probation, or if the prior offense was similar to the current offense. Some examples of crimes calculated pursuant to the foregoing are careless or reckless driving, disorderly conduct, contempt of court, gambling, prostitution, or trespassing. Further, cases that ended in diversion or deferred prosecution usually will not add points. The exception is cases in which the defendant entered a formal plea of guilty or nolo contendere (no contest) and a different, agreed upon sentence would be assessed if a defendant breached the diversion or deferred prosecution.

A prior sentence, which punished criminal conduct that is part of the current offense, does not count as points against the defendant. For example, when a defendant is prosecuted in both state and federal court for the same conduct, the defendant will not receive any points for the prior state offense.

Sentences imposed in foreign countries do not count. Sentences for expunged, reversed, or invalid convictions do not count. Likewise, sentences that are "set aside" for errors of law, including and especially when the defendant's innocence is determined post-conviction, do not count. More often than not, prior sentences for offenses committed by the defendant prior to his or her eighteenth (18) birthday do not count, except when a juvenile is sentenced as an adult to a term of thirteen (13) months or more. Sentences imposed on juveniles also count if the defendant *began* the current offense within five (5) years of completing his or her juvenile sentence.

Perhaps most important to the Criminal History Category analysis is the inclusion of prior criminal conduct that resulted in a withhold of adjudication by the sentencing court. For all other intents and purposes, the criminal conduct would not be attached to the defendant's criminal history; however, under the *Federal Sentencing Guidelines*, a withhold of adjudication acts as a conviction and the subject's criminal conduct is evaluated as all other convictions are under the guidelines.

———•———

CHAPTER 2

RECOMMENDATION BARGAINING

———•———

Recommendation bargaining, also known as "sentencing bargaining," is the entering of a plea in return for a simple non-binding recommendation from the prosecutor that gives the defendant less than any other bargain. With regard to any sentencing recommendation or agreed upon sentence, the advisory guidelines instruct that the court should not follow the recommendation or accept the plea agreement unless the sentence falls within the applicable sentencing guideline range or departs from that range for justifiable reasons. (USSG § 6B1.2(b).) Post-*Booker*, this provision can no longer be considered binding on sentencing courts because not only are the guidelines no longer mandatory, but also the provision itself reflects the old, pre-*Booker* sentencing regime, where justifiable departures were the only ones permitted by the guidelines. Now, of course, the court must consider a broader array of factors under Section 3553(a) in determining the "justified" sentence. Indeed, even in our pre-*Booker* world, some courts refused to consider this guideline provision as binding on a sentencing court.

SECTION 1

PRE-INDICTMENT

———•———

In the pre-indictment context, before a matter is assigned to a particular judge, both sides have greater incentive to negotiate a resolution pursuant to Federal Rule of Criminal Procedure 11(c)(1)(C), which provides for a binding agreement with regard to a particular sentence or sentencing factor. If the judge refuses to accept the agreement, the defendant may withdraw the plea pursuant to Federal Rule of Criminal Procedure 11(c)(5)(B).

Post-*Booker*, the government, in many instances, is more willing to discuss a binding plea agreement in order to achieve greater certainty regarding the ultimate sentence. From a defense perspective, such certainty can be an appealing feature. It is important to remember that the rule permits a binding agreement with regard to sentencing factors like the advisory guideline range. Even where the parties cannot agree on an ultimate sentence, it is often worth exploring whether you can agree on the guideline score, or even a guideline factor (like the absence of a role adjustment for an organizer or leader).

Nevertheless, the real challenge is trying to get the government to agree to a sentence that is below the otherwise applicable guideline range. The best approach is to try and convince the government that a reasonable alternative guideline calculation can be made so that the agreed upon sentence is within the guideline range. There may also be guideline departures that permit the government to accept the defendant's desired sentencing range as consistent with the guidelines.

SECTION 2

USING A WAIVER OF RIGHTS AS A BARGAINING CHIP

———•———

Where the government is unwilling to consider a binding agreement with regard to sentencing factors or an ultimate sentence, one must then discuss what the government is willing to recommend, or at least not oppose. In such instances, the government will often request either:

(1) a stipulation that a sentence within the guideline range is one, but not necessarily the only, "reasonable" sentence, or

(2) that the defendant waive his or her right to appeal any sentence.

The former language, without an appellate waiver, dramatically reduces, if not eliminates, any hope to obtain a sentence outside of the guideline range because the stipulation means that any guideline sentence is essentially immune from challenge on appeal.

Post-*Booker*, an appellate waiver by both the government and the defense may prove advantageous to defendants. Where the defense has a strong argument for a downward departure under the guidelines, an appellate waiver by the government may cause a sentencing judge to consider the request more favorably, given that there is no risk of being embarrassed in the court of appeals. This is a somewhat risky strategy given the possibility that you will not be able to challenge a sentence above the advisory guideline range as set forth in the plea agreement. That said, in the appropriate case, and purely as a strategic move approved by the defendant, where the mitigating factors are strong and where you know the sentencing history and practices of the judge, it may be a risk worth taking.

SECTION 3

MINIMUM/MANDATORY SENTENCES

Minimum/Mandatory sentences are exactly what they say: the minimum allowable punishment for a certain crime is mandatory. I can understand the confusion of "mandatory" having discussed earlier that *Booker* made the Guidelines "advisory," rather than mandatory, but the two concepts are mutually exclusive. Mandatory sentencing laws require binding prison terms of a particular length for people convicted of certain federal crimes. These inflexible, "one-size-fits-all" sentencing laws may seem like a quick-fix solution for crime, but I would agree Minimum/Mandatory sentences prevent judges from fitting the punishment to the individual and the circumstances of their offenses. In other words, if a defendant only scores 70 months after the Sentencing Guidelines calculation, but his crime carries a Minimum/Mandatory sentence, then the defendant receives the Minimum/*Mandatory* sentence from the Judge. Most Minimum/Mandatory sentences apply to drug offenses, but Congress has enacted them for other crimes, including certain gun, pornography, and economic offenses.

For defendants facing statutory mandatory minimum sentences, *Booker* does not directly provide the district court with any greater discretion to sentence a defendant below the statutory minimum sentence. However, two mechanisms exist for such defendants to obtain below minimum sentences. The first is cooperating to receive a downward departure for substantial assistance, pursuant to U.S.S.G. § 5K1.1, or a post-sentence reduction under Federal Rule of Criminal Procedure 35 (discussed in more length later). The incentive to cooperate remains largely unchanged for those defendants facing statutory mandatory minimum sentences who are not eligible for the "safety valve," which is the second mechanism, 18 U.S.C. § 3553(f), because substantial assistance motions provide the only realistic mechanism to obtain a sentence significantly below the minimum statutory sentence. (See 18 U.S.C. § 3553(e).)

The "safety valve" provides the second mechanism that might provide a defendant with the opportunity for a below-minimum sentence. The safety valve provides first time offenders who meet the criteria set forth in 18 U.S.C. § 3553(f) and U.S.S.G. § 5C1.2 with the opportunity to be sentenced below the statutory minimum mandatory sentence.

Post-*Booker*, the safety valve may provide more substantial relief to qualifying persons.

When the guidelines were mandatory, safety valve defendants were sentenced within the guideline range because of the application of the guideline provision irrespective of the mandatory minimum sentence. However, post-*Booker*, the guidelines must be treated as advisory. A sentencing court is free to sentence a safety valve defendant to whatever sentence is appropriate after consideration of the 18 U.S.C. § 3553(a) factors without regard to the statutory minimum sentence.

For defendants not facing mandatory minimum sentences, cooperation plea agreements need to be evaluated carefully by defense counsel. In the pre-*Booker* world, where the guideline sentence was mandatory, many defendants depended on cooperation as the only potential avenue for a below-guideline sentence. Now, of course, the advisory guidelines are only one part of the sentencing calculation and a Section 5K1.1 motion is not required for a below-guideline sentence. In addition, some courts have held that the defendant may receive credit for cooperation even where the government does not file a motion for substantial assistance.

SECTION 4

COURT IS NOT BOUND BY ANY AGREEMENT

————•————

Non-binding recommendations are authorized under Rule 11(c)(1)(B). USSG §6B1.2(b) authorizes, but does not require, the court to accept the recommendation if it is within the applicable guideline range or departs for justifiable reasons. When confronted with a recommendation or a cap below the guidelines, some courts simply recite the mantra that the sentence departs for justifiable reasons and go ahead and accept the deal. Unfortunately, the commentary to USSG §6B1.2(b) notes that departing for justifiable reasons actually means that such departure is authorized by 18 U.S.C. §3553(b). That statute requires the court to impose a sentence within the guideline range unless there exists an aggravating or mitigating circumstance not adequately considered by the Sentencing Commission. In other words, the words "justifiable reasons" in the Guideline do not create a new reason for departure, as the facts of the case must be sufficient to justify a departure under the normal rules.

Where there is no right to withdraw from a plea such as where the plea agreement is for a recommendation under Rule 11(c)(1)(B) the court should advise the defendant that he has no subsequent right to withdraw if the government's recommendation is rejected. Rule 11(c)(3)(B). *Failure to so advise* has been held to be a reversible error unless the record shows the defendant possessed that knowledge; however, there are a number of exceptions. For example, failure to advise the defendant that she would not be allowed to withdraw her guilty plea if the court rejected the government's sentencing recommendation was error, but when the court did in fact follow the recommendation, there was no prejudice and the sentence was affirmed. A similar failure to advise the defendant during the colloquy was harmless where, at sentencing, the court became aware of the problem and gave the defendant the opportunity to withdraw and the defendant refused.

In practice, the government rarely recommends departures, other than USSG §5K.1 departures for substantial assistance; instead, the common practice with respect to recommendation bargaining is limited to sentences within the guideline range, or to a limited set of departures. Routine departures include those for substantial assistance and those under fast-track programs (discussed later). At the very least, assuming you have been above board with the prosecution, they may just stand silently at their table, which should tip the judge in your favor.

SECTION 5

EFFECT OF RECOMMENDATION BELOW THE GUIDELINE RANGE

The Guidelines require the court to reject a plea outside the guideline range unless there is justification for a departure under 18 U.S.C. 3553(b) and the Guidelines themselves. Nonetheless, if the court accepts a recommendation and sentence below the guideline range, that decision may be shielded from appellate scrutiny by the doctrine of waiver. After all, the fact that the prosecution has recommended the sentence should lead the court and the defendant to reasonably expect that the government would not appeal the sentence. A contrary result would be troubling for the appellate courts because the parties would in effect create their own self-help departure scheme. Courts have held in numerous cases that a defendant waives any objection that he fails to make in the district court. One would expect the same rule to apply to the government.

The government's failure to recommend a sentence at the low end of the guideline range, as called for by a plea agreement, ended with an appellate reversal even where the prosecutor admitted that she was recommending the low end. Contrarily, in a case where the written plea agreement contained substance of the government's recommendation and the appellate court felt that if the government had made the recommendation in court at the time of sentencing it would not have likely changed the defendant's sentence. Nevertheless, an agreement to recommend a sentence does not imply an obligation to do so enthusiastically or to set forth on the record the reasons for the recommendation. The prosecutor may not pay lip service to the agreement with a recommendation, but in the same breath undermine that recommendation by supporting the higher presentence report guideline calculation in a sentencing memo. In such a situation, Courts may end up ordering specific performance via resentencing, noting that while the recommendation need not be made with any particular degree of enthusiasm. In all events, it is unfair for the prosecutor to inject material reservations about an agreement to which the government has committed itself.

By way of further example, where the defendant pleaded guilty in federal court with an agreement that the government would recommend concurrent time with an upcoming federal sentencing in another state, and where the government attorney in that other state in fact requested a consecutive sentence, the defendant was entitled to specific performance from the government because any promises made by an Assistant United States Attorney (AUSA) in one district will bind an AUSA in another district. Further, even an impossible promise must be kept. Where the government agreed to recommend probation, but probation was not permissible under the guidelines, and the government informed the court that it was not bound to impose a sentence that would be illegal under the guidelines, the plea bargain was based on an unfulfillable promise and the defendant should be allowed to withdraw his plea.

CHAPTER 3

STIPULATION BARGAINING

———•———

Stipulation bargaining; the entering of a plea in return for a binding recommendation is the holy grail of plea bargaining in federal court. Armed with a stipulated sentence, a client can be assured of what is going to happen, unless the judge rejects the plea altogether.

SECTION 1

RULES AND GUIDELINES

———•———

Bargaining for stipulated sentences is authorized under Rule 11 (c)(1)(C) and is analyzed for Sentencing Guidelines purposes under §6B1.2(c). The judge may accept the agreement if the sentence is within the guideline range or departs for justifiable reasons, meaning that there is a legally sufficient reason for departure. Rule 11(c)(5) refers to the right to withdraw provided by the rules and the guidelines in the case of Rule 11(c)(1)(A) and 11(c)(1)(C) agreements. This is the only sense in which a plea agreement including a stipulation is binding on the court. The court need not accept it, but the defendant will be allowed to withdraw if the court does not.

SENTENCE AGREEMENTS UNDER RULE 11(C)(1)(C)

Often the plea agreement will not stipulate an exact sentence, but will instead set forth a maximum often called a cap or a range of sentence. Prior to the amendments of 1999, the rule only provided for the stipulation of a specific sentence. The rule now provides for stipulation of a sentencing range. The court can always reject a plea under Rule 11(c)(5) and the guidelines require it to do so if the plea is outside the guideline range unless a departure is justified; however, if the agreement is under Rule 11(c)(1)(C), the court must either accept the agreement or allow the defendant to withdraw from the plea. Under these circumstances, the court is under some pressure to go ahead and accept the agreement and sentence below the guideline range. The possibility of a waiver of appeal by the government would also apply in this instance.

The 1999 amendments to Rule 11(c)(1) now permit the government to recommend or stipulate whether a particular provision of the guidelines, policy statement, or sentencing factor applies in a particular case. Recommendations under Rule 11(c)(1)(B) are never binding, and the defendant has no recourse if the court rejects them. Rejection of stipulations under Rule 11(c)(1)(C), however, gives rise to a right to withdraw the plea under Rule 11(c)(5).

SECTION 2

COURT MUST REJECT INACCURATE STIPULATIONS

———•———

Generally, USSG §6B1.4(d) states that sentencing courts are not bound by stipulations in plea agreements but instead are free to determine the facts relevant to sentencing. The court may, and often times will, rely on the presentence report to determine the true facts. The idea that the government stipulated to certain facts in the plea agreement does not prevent the district court from considering conduct outside the stipulated facts, including uncharged conduct. However, if the government argues a position contrary to its stipulation, as opposed to the judge simply rejecting it, there may be a violation of the plea agreement.

———•———

SECTION 3

STIPULATIONS THAT HURT THE DEFENDANT MAY BE RELIED UPON

———•———

Stipulations that go against the defendant can be relied upon by the court even if they are not supported by the presentence report apparently as admissions of a party. Even stipulations regarding dismissed counts may be considered. In determining relevant conduct, the district court could properly rely on a stipulation in the plea agreement that certain conduct constitutes relevant conduct under § 1B1.3 of the guidelines. In other words, the court ignores the defense argument that some conduct is not truly relevant, and instead relies on the stipulation that it was indeed relevant. Similarly, the defendant's stipulation the abuse of trust enhancement should apply, coupled with an agreement not to appeal the accuracy of the stipulated facts, constituted a waiver of the right to appeal a finding based thereon. Therefore, a stipulation may constitute a waiver, under appropriate circumstances, but it does not relieve the court of its obligation to determine its own view of the facts and law.

———•———

CHAPTER 4

PLEA AGREEMENTS INVOLVING COOPERATION

———— • •————

In reality, the name of the game in federal court is cooperation. Defendants who proceed to trial, and who are convicted, face sentences that are sometimes ten times longer than the sentences imposed on similarly-situated defendants who cooperate with the government. More often than not, the government will start their investigation and case at the bottom of the conspiracy. In other words, the government doesn't go after the boss; instead, they go after the everyday, low-level conspirators, charge them with the crime(s), and essentially force them to choose between cooperating and a lengthy prison sentence. From there, the government infiltrates the target conspiracy group level by level until they reach the top.

———— • •————

SECTION 1

DON'T BE LATE
BE THE FIRST TO COOPERATE

———— • ————

From a defense attorney prospective, it is critical the prospect of cooperation is brought up with the defendant at the earliest possible opportunity. Because most federal criminal cases are multi-defendant, the usual course of events is that the defendant who contacts the prosecution first will be rewarded and receive preferential treatment over the next defendant who comes calling. This is based, in part, on the idea of cumulative information. In other words, the government won't reward defendant B, C, or D for the same information already provided by defendant A. Further, as discussed at greater length above, in the event a defendant is facing a Minimum/Mandatory sentence, and he or she is otherwise eligible for the "Safety Valve," cooperation is required as part of the safety valve consideration. It is true that cooperation for purposes of the safety valve is distinguishable from common cooperation, *i.e.*, the defendant need only to be forthright with information concerning *his or her conduct*, and there is no requirement to provide information about others that are of interest to the prosecution. That being said, the defendant should cooperate with the government beyond just his or her conduct because the government's agreement, or rather non-objection, to a safety valve request will go a long way to persuading the

Judge at sentencing to grant the safety valve request and order a sentence more commensurate with the sentencing guidelines score.

"Cooperation" is simply a euphemism for providing information, and perhaps testimony, to the government about other individuals. The concept is also called "substantial assistance" for sentencing guideline purposes. Typically, this process involves "debriefings" with federal agents, and can mean testimony against other individuals. The government, to the greatest extent possible, will keep the identities of the cooperating defendant(s) secret, typically by sealing all records in the court file of the cooperator's case so that other potential defendants and attorneys cannot see the details of the cooperator, including his or her name. In the event that one or more of the non-cooperators intends to proceed to trial, the government may disclose the identities and the statements of cooperating defendants in the time leading up to trial as part of the discovery phase.

Whether or not to cooperate is an extremely difficult decision for defendants. To the naked eye, the decision to cooperate is a no brainer; tell what you know and save yourself from a harsh prison sentence. However, there is much more to this decision, and the defendant, when approached to cooperate, doesn't think logically like the layman would; rather, they start to process how they may be called upon to testify against others involved in the criminal activity, some of who may be very dangerous. They think about whether their decision may put their friends and family in danger by those who will be hurt by the cooperation. Also, "snitches" or "rats" as they are called, (think Mafia) are not treated well in prison by other inmates. Prison is an unpleasant enough place when you don't have to constantly look over your shoulder because you are known as a cooperator.

SECTION 2

SUBJECT MATTER OF COOPERATION

Sample Plea Agreement Language: Defendant agrees to cooperate fully with the United States in the investigation and prosecution of other persons, and to testify, subject to prosecution for perjury or making a false statement, fully and truthfully before any federal court proceeding or federal grand jury in connection with the charges in this case and other matters, such cooperation to further include a full and complete disclosure of all relevant information, including production of any and all books, papers, documents, and other objects in the Defendant's possession or control, and to be reasonably available for interviews, which the United States may require.

This appears to be extremely broad. Defense attorneys should inquire whether this language limits testimony to trials that are related to the offense for which the defendant was charged, or be against anyone or any case about which the defendant has provided information. In a situation where the defendant has cooperated *pre-sentence* and is asked to cooperate *post-sentence* pursuant to the above vague language, he or she may refuse to further cooperate without further penalty. This often happens when a defendant feels his or her sentence did not adequately reflect the level of *pre-sentence* cooperation (imagine that!). Nevertheless, the defendant could be found in breach of his or her cooperation obligations because of the vagueness of the plea language. To limit the defendant's exposure, it is important to agree upon and advise the defendant of the scope of this commitment prior to executing the plea agreement.

Most agreements with a cooperating defendant are similar across the country, although it is often possible to stipulate to an agreement that does not require the giving of information or testimony against family members or certain persons who may have threatened the defendant in the past. As can be expected, in order to grant any special requests from a defendant, the prosecution would need to feel that the defendant's level of cooperation was strong enough to warrant such leeway.

SECTION 3

UNDERCOVER WORK

———— • ————

Sample Plea Agreement Language: Defendant will not work undercover without the permission and supervision of government agents.

Prosecutors often say that this provision is to prevent free-lance work, usually drug or arms sales activity by the defendant, which the defendant later claims to have performed on behalf of the government. But, does this provision imply that the defendant has agreed to work undercover? If so, to what extent? Does he have to set up drug deals, or merely be present? Is there a requirement to wear a recording device such as a wire or small camera? These kinds of details should be worked out ahead of time and put in writing to avoid misunderstandings since the defendant and prosecution essentially work together.

SECTION 4

USE OF INFORMATION AGAINST DEFENDANT

Sample Plea Agreement Language: The United States agrees that no self-incriminating information, which the defendant may provide during the course of the defendant's cooperation and pursuant to this agreement, shall be used in determining the applicable guideline range.

The Guideline range will be calculated with the government's proof independent of the defendant's cooperation. USSG §1B1.8(a) prevents the use of information provided by the defendant pursuant to a cooperation agreement to determine the guideline range if the government has agreed not to use it, as the government does in the sample agreement above. In the absence of a USSG §1B1.8(a) agreement not to use information, boilerplate language in a plea agreement saying that the government was free to provide all relevant information to the court at sentencing was held to override the Rule 410 and Rule 11(f) protection of statements made during a proffer in plea negotiations, even though the proffer agreement itself provided that the information would not be used. Essentially, defendants can provide information through cooperation knowing they may incriminate themselves, but won't be penalized for it at sentencing. It's difficult enough for defendants to agree to cooperate as it is, let alone fearing they will be penalized for telling the entire truth.

Unfortunately, some courts have decided that although the information cannot be used to determine the guideline range, it can and should be used to determine if a sentence is reasonable in a post-*Booker* analysis. The courts are relying on 18 USC § 3661, which says that no limitation shall be placed on the information the court may receive and consider for purposes of sentencing. Also, not all information provided by the defendant is protected. USSG §1B1.8(b) specifically allows use of the information if it was already known to the government, if it is about prior convictions and is used to determine criminal history or career offender status, if it is to be used in a perjury prosecutions, if there has been a breach by defendant, or to determine if a downward departure for substantial assistance is warranted. The information must have been provided as part of the cooperation, as opposed to statements made to a probation officer in a routine interview, which are not protected under USSG §1B1.8(a).

There is a distinction between information provided pursuant to a cooperation agreement and statements made during failed plea negotiations. The protection of USSG

§1B1.8(a) is contingent on government *agreement*, unlike the protections of Rule 410 of the Federal Rules of Evidence and Rule 11(f) of the Federal Rules of Criminal Procedure, all of which prohibit the use of statements made in the course of plea discussions with an attorney for the prosecuting authority, which do not result in a guilty plea.

SECTION 5

TYPES OF PROMISES
MADE BY THE GOVERNMENT

Sample Plea Agreement Language: At the conclusion of defendant's cooperation, pursuant to this agreement, the United States will, at the time of sentencing, pursuant to Title 18, United States Code, Section 3553(e), Title 28, United States Code, Section 994(n) and Sentencing Guidelines §5K1.1, move that the court depart from the Guidelines and any applicable minimum sentence established by law to reflect the defendant's substantial assistance in the investigation and prosecution. The United States will also bring the nature and extent of the defendant's cooperation to the attention of the court, and the Bureau of Prisons, if applicable, at sentencing or any other appropriate time. The United States retains the right to make a sentencing recommendation, including a recommendation that the defendant receive a maximum possible sentence provided for under this agreement. The United States further retains the right to allocute at the time of sentencing. The defendant understands that the United States will bring to the attention of the court all pertinent facts concerning his or her participation in any criminal activity, and all facts affecting the sentencing guidelines calculations.

In a cooperation agreement, the government may make several kinds of promises. Most importantly, the government may promise to make a motion for downward departure under USSG §5K1.1 for substantial assistance. This is commonly referred to as a "5K Motion." Section 5K1.1 of the Sentencing Guidelines provides that, upon motion by the Government, a court may depart from the guideline range. A substantial assistance motion must be based on assistance that is substantial to the Government's case. It is not appropriate to utilize substantial assistance motions as a case management tool to secure plea agreements and avoid trials. Without this motion, there is no benefit to the defendant to cooperate, in most cases.

In order to permit departure below a statutory mandatory minimum, the government must also move for departure pursuant to 18 U.S.C. §3553(e). In all events, the government's motion attests to the defendant's substantial assistance in a criminal investigation and further requests that the district court depart *below* the minimum of the applicable guideline sentencing range. The government should also agree to bring the defendant's cooperation to the court's attention, including at least all of the criteria that 26 USSG §5K1.1(a) lists as significant, such as truthfulness, completeness, reliability, nature and extent of assistance, injury or danger to the defendant or his or her family, and timeliness. However, after the government has made the departure motions, downward departure by the court is discretionary, not mandatory, and the appellate court has no jurisdiction to review the trial court's discretionary decision to refuse downward departure under §5K1.1. In other words, there appears to be no appellate relief if the defendant gets a §5K1.1 motion from the prosecution, but the court refuses to depart. So, defendants: no cooperator's remorse. It is a risk that defendants must take in order to give themselves a chance at a lesser sentence, but is by no means a guarantee.

If, on the other hand, the government promises to make such a motion, but fails to do so there may be relief under only certain circumstances. The government may also reserve the right to make a recommendation based on the cooperation. Where possible this should be within a specific negotiated range. Further, the government may agree to a cap under Rule 11(c)(1)(C), something not done in the above sample language. If the plea is under Rule 11(e)(1)(C), setting forth a specific sentence, the judge must honor the agreement or allow the defendant to withdraw. This is always important, and may become more important if there is a breach of the agreement. Note that a provision like the one above saying that the government was free to provide all relevant information to the court at sentencing was held to override the protected nature of statements made during a proffer in plea negotiations, even though the proffer agreement itself provided that the information would not be used. Under the same theory, namely that the plea agreement contract modifies any previous agreements, the government could possibly provide the court with information gained during cooperation under a promise of confidentiality.

SECTION 6

TIMING OF SENTENCING PROCEEDINGS

———— • ————

Sample Plea Agreement Language: The plea of guilty shall be entered as soon as practicable, but the sentencing on the guilty plea will be deferred, with consent of the court, for a period of one year from the entry of the guilty plea, and upon motion of the government and concurrence of the court, for a period beyond that one year. It is the intention of the parties that sentencing on the instant charges be postponed until such time as defendant's cooperation and all related forfeiture actions have been completed.

The agreement provides that sentencing will be delayed for the benefit of both parties. Often times, an agreement will be struck years before, filed under seal to protect to cooperator, and the government will continue to make its case against other targets. This is a win/win; the government wants time for the defendant to work, and the defendant wants more work to be considered by the court. This is not an exact science, and by no means is the court bound by this agreement. After all, leaving cases open on a judge's docket is a good way to land yourself in the doghouse. The court can, at its discretion, refuse a continuance past one year and can force sentencing to go forward.

———— • ————

SECTION 7

DETERMINATION OF BREACH OF AGREEMENT

Sample Plea Agreement Language: If there is a dispute regarding the obligations of the parties under this agreement, the United States District Court shall determine whether the United States or the defendant has failed to comply with this agreement including whether the defendant has been truthful. Nothing shall limit the United States' methods of verifying the truthfulness of the defendant's statements. As part of this process, in the sole discretion of the United States, the defendant agrees to submit to a polygraph examination to verify any information the defendant may provide to the United States, including but not limited to the defendant's assets. Such examination will be conducted by a polygrapher chosen and conducted in a manner determined in the sole discretion of the United States. Neither party shall object to the admissibility in evidence of the results of such examination in any proceeding to enforce or set aside this agreement in which compliance with the terms of this agreement are an issue.

The foregoing sample agreement language allows the government to require a polygraph exam. It does not condition the agreement on passing the exam, but it does make the exam admissible at a hearing on compliance. Polygraphs are inadmissible in state and federal courts absent strict findings or agreements, and that is because polygraphs have been found unreliable. To protect the defendant, the defense should try to insert language into the agreement that allows it's own polygraph evidence.

The typical breach in cooperation cases is failure to testify truthfully. The agreement provides that the court makes the final determination on failure to comply. Other forms of this type of agreement require the government to make a "good faith" determination on truthfulness, which may also lead to a hearing. For example, before the government may decline to fulfill its obligations under a plea agreement, it must establish the defendant's breach by a preponderance of the evidence. The burden of proof on whether the agreement was breached is generally on the person alleging the breach. However, the burden can, in a sense, be reversed in a substantial assistance case. Where the defendant is claiming that the government breached the agreement by failing to move for assistance, the defendant may have to first demonstrate by a preponderance of the evidence that he provided the degree of assistance contemplated by the agreement.

When information has been proffered (provided) by the defendant, and the government contends that the cooperation agreement has been breached, they will seek to use the information against the defendant. This is not, however, automatic relief and the client is still entitled to due process prior to use of the information. The most common reasons for the government contending that the client has breached the proffer agreement are (a) the failure to provide completely truthful information and (b) the failure to fully disclose information. Partial disclosure as well as untruthful information can (and will!) breach the terms of the proffer.

Many proffer and cooperation agreements contain a paragraph providing that in the event the government contends that the client has breached the agreement, the government will provide notice to the defendant prior to the attempted use of information. This type of agreement also provides that prior to the government's attempted use of the information, the defendant will be entitled to a hearing at which time the government must establish a breach of the cooperation agreement by a preponderance of the evidence standard. Even if the agreement does not contain such language, the defendant's attorney should insist that, as a matter of due process, the defendant is entitled to such a hearing. If the government is successful at such a hearing, then all the information provided in the proffer session is fair game for the government to use in any proceeding. In the event of a trial, the information provided during the proffer session would permit the government to know what the defendant will say, if he or she testifies, and to use the proffered information for impeachment purposes if the defendant offers testimony that is different or conflicting than what was provided in the proffer session.

SECTION 8

PENALTIES FOR BREACH BY DEFENDANT

Sample Plea Agreement Language: If the defendant fails to comply with any obligation or promise pursuant to this agreement, the United States may:

1) In its sole discretion, declare any provision of this agreement null and void in accordance with [the paragraph calling for the court to determine the breach] and the defendant understands that he or she will not be permitted to withdraw his or her plea of guilty made in connection with this agreement;

2) Indict and prosecute the defendant for any offense known to the United States for which he is responsible, including all offenses committed pursuant to his/her failure to cooperate, and the defendant waives any statute of limitations, Speedy Trial Act and constitutional restrictions on bringing charges after the execution of this agreement;

3) Argue for a maximum sentence for the offenses to which the defendant has plead guilty;

4) Use in any prosecution any information, statements, documents and evidence provided by the defendant both before and after the plea agreement including derivative evidence; and

5) Advise the Bureau of Prisons that the defendant is no longer a cooperating witness, and recommend classifying the defendant in a higher custodial level.

The agreement indicates that "any provision" may be declared null by the government, subject to review of the alleged breach by the court. The Double Jeopardy Clause does not prevent setting aside a plea and reinstating charges in the event of a breach, but the government's remedies appear to be limited by several cases. For example, the above language says that the defendant cannot withdraw the plea, however, if the plea is under Rule 11(c)(1)(C), then the judge must honor the agreement or allow the defendant to withdraw. It also says that the government can use any information provided by the defendant against the defendant, but several courts have prevented such use where the breach was failure to pass a polygraph, in the absence of a specific agreement to allow such use. Nonetheless, the crux of this type of agreement is clearly that all benefit will be lost in the event of a breach by the defendant, and it theoretically serves as a deterrent to the defendant and a safety net for the government.

SECTION 9

REMEDIES FOR BREACH BY GOVERNMENT

When the prosecution breaches a plea agreement, the breach may be remedied by either specific performance of the agreement or by allowing the defendant to withdraw the plea. Discretion and interpretation still exist on this side of the fence as well. For example, the government agrees to file a 5K motion if the defendant provides substantial assistance; the government's failure to do so after determining that the assistance was not substantial is not a breach. Such refusals are reviewed by the district court only on a limited basis, to determine if the refusal was arbitrary or was based on an unconstitutional motive or in bad-faith.

An example of bad-faith would be where the government agrees to recommend a reduction if the defendant is truthful when debriefed by agents, the government's failure to debrief the defendant prior to his sentencing is a breach of the agreement, particularly where the debriefing could have allowed the defendant to satisfy the one remaining requirement necessary for safety valve protection. The government's agreement to move for 5K1.1 departure if the defendant provided substantial assistance obligated the government to give the defendant the opportunity to furnish such assistance. Although the defendant changed his or her plea to nolo contendere and was denying knowledge of much of the criminal activity, the government knew that when it amended the plea agreement to allow the nolo plea. The amended agreement still included the substantial assistance provision and thus the government was obligated to carry through and allow the defendant to try to cooperate, i.e., that the defendant make full, truthful disclosure to the government no later than sentencing.

Where the government agreed to present a Rule 35 motion (similar to a 5K Motion except it is *post* sentencing) detailing the extent of the defendant's cooperation, but details of the cooperation were not presented in the motion for safety reasons and the court refused to grant an evidentiary hearing on the motion, the government was effectively prevented from presenting the Rule 35 motion and the plea agreement was deemed breached.

SECTION 10

AGREEMENTS REGARDING DEPORTATION

In 2012, the government put in place what is called the Fast Track Program. The basic premise of the Fast Track Program is that, within an expedited time frame, a qualifying defendant in an illegal re-entry case must plead guilty. Under the plea agreement, a defendant will be required to give up certain rights. In exchange for the above, the Government may agree to move at sentencing for a downward departure from the adjusted base offense level found by the District Court (after application of the adjustment for acceptance of responsibility) of a specific number of levels, not to exceed 4 levels.

The defendant must enter into a written plea agreement that includes at least the following terms wherein the defendant agrees to:

(a) A factual basis that accurately reflects his or her offense conduct;

(b) Not file any of the motions described in Rule 12(b)(3), Fed. R. Crim. P. iii;

(c) Waive appeal, and

(d) Waive the opportunity to challenge his or her conviction under 28 U.S.C. § 2255, except on the issue of ineffective assistance of counsel.

The Fast Track Program is designed to reduce unwarranted geographic disparity and to increase efficiency in illegal re-entry cases under Title 8 U.S.C. § 1326. While Fast Track Programs have previously been implemented in some judicial districts, the government is now implementing a uniform nationwide policy.

—————•—————

PART 3

PENALTIES, THE CONSEQUENCES OF ERRORS, AND PARTY ACCEPTANCE

The government of the United States is and always has been a lawyer's government."

~ Chauncey Depew, Esq. (1834 –1928)

PENALTIES, THE CONSEQUENCES OF ERRORS, AND PARTY ACCEPTANCE

—— • ——

The sentencing and penalty phase is without a doubt the most nerve wracking part of any criminal case for a defendant. This is the part that is on the defendant and his or her family's mind from the start, *i.e.*, what are they facing, how much "time" could they do. From a defense attorney perspective, the work you put into limiting the defendant's exposure will make or break the case. Indeed, one error, no matter how minor, can hurt your client for the rest of his or her life.

CHAPTER 1

PENALTIES

———•———

The penalties Section of a plea agreement sets forth the maximum penalties that the law allows for the charge to which the defendant will plead. Its only real functions are to make sure that the defendant has been properly advised of the penalties and to inform the judge of what to tell the defendant at the change of plea hearing.

Sample Plea Agreement Language: a) A violation of Title 21 U.S.C. §841(a)(1) and §841(b)(1)(A)(vii), is punishable by a mandatory minimum term of imprisonment of ten years, and a maximum term of imprisonment of up to life, or a maximum fine of $4,000,000 or both. b) According to the Sentencing Guidelines, the court shall order the defendant to:

1) Make restitution to any victims of the offense, unless, pursuant to Title 18, U.S.C. §3663, the court determines that restitution would not be appropriate, and

2) Pay a fine, unless, pursuant to Section 5E1.2(f) of the Guidelines, the defendant establishes the applicability of the exceptions found therein.

Furthermore, the following considerations are given:

1) Pursuant to Title 18 U.S.C. §3583, to serve a term of supervised release when required by law or when a sentence of imprisonment of more than one year is imposed, the court may impose a term of supervised released in all other cases;

2) Pursuant to Title 18 U.S.C. §§3561-3566, §3559, the defendant may not be sentenced to a period of probation; and

3) Pursuant to Title 18 §3013, the court is required to impose a special assessment on the defendant of $100.00 per count.

SECTION 1

COMMON ERRORS IN PENALTY TERMS

Don't take the plea agreement language setting forth the penalty terms at face value—after all, the government drafted it. Maximum incarceration terms are usually correct, as they are set out in the statutes. Mandatory minimum terms must be checked carefully, particularly in drug, gun and Continuing Criminal Enterprise (CCE) cases. Authorized supervised release terms are often wrong. In general, they are controlled by 18 U.S.C. §3583, which in turn relies on the classification of the offense under 18 U.S.C. §3559. Specific statutes sometimes have their own supervised release requirements, such as the drug statute 21 U.S.C. §841. Authorized fine amounts are often wrong. Fines for offenses before the guidelines went into effect are controlled by the specific statute. Guideline case fines are controlled by the greater of the specific statute or the fine in 18 U.S.C. §3571, which was amended in December of 1987 to change the misdemeanor fines. The general fine statute relies on the classification of the offense under 18 U.S.C. §3559. Special assessments are controlled by 18 U.S.C. §3013, which provides for smaller assessments for class A, B, and C misdemeanors. The Section was amended in 1996 to provide for $100, as opposed to $50, assessments for felonies.

SECTION 2

EFFECT OF ERRORS IN PENALTY TERMS

Rule 11(c)(1) requires that defendants be advised of the mandatory minimum provided by the law, if any, and the maximum possible penalty including the effect of special parole or supervised release. Many mistakes in advising defendants are considered "harmless errors," generally because the defendant receives a sentence well below the maximum. For example, it has been held as a harmless error where the defendant was misadvised that the maximum sentence was life imprisonment and he ultimately received 15 years sentence and a 5-year term of supervised release.

However, courts may find harmful error where the combination of sentences received could cause the defendant's liberty to be restricted beyond the maximum sentences advised prior to sentencing, such as where a defendant was not advised of the possibility of supervised release and received maximum term *and* maximum supervised release. Also, advising a defendant that he was subject to a 5-year mandatory minimum at arraignment, and then finding him responsible for more cocaine at sentencing, triggering a mandatory 10-year sentence, invalidated his guilty plea.

Failure to mention restitution during the plea colloquy was found to be a harmless error, where the defendant was made aware of the restitution obligation through his plea and cooperation agreements. It was also a harmless error where the defendant was advised of a possible fine, but not of possible restitution, and the restitution imposed was less than the fine could have ultimately been. The remedy in some cases for a bad penalty advisement has been a direction by the appellate court that the district court vacates the part of the sentence that exceeds the advisement, rather than allowing the defendant to withdraw his plea. There may also be, and should be, an error where it appears that the decision to plead was impacted by the erroneous advice given by the court. For example, the defendant's guilty plea and waiver of trial was invalid in a situation where:

(a) the defendant was told at arraignment that he faced 60 years for two drug counts,

(b) but he actually faced only 30 years,

(c) he then pled guilty to one of the counts in return for dismissal of the other,

(d) the court thought he was subject to 30 years, which he was not, and

(e) sentenced him to 15 years.

SECTION 3

FACTUAL BASIS

————— • —————

The factual basis Section establishes that there are sufficient facts to support a conviction. The defendant admits the truth of these facts as a precursor to the plea. Very rarely does the defendant get to barter and the government is the author of the factual basis. These facts may also form the basis of some of the probation officer's guideline calculations and must be examined carefully. Rule 11(b)(3) requires the court to determine that there is a factual basis for the plea.

As mentioned in other Sections, stipulation within a factual basis to a greater offense may require the use of the guideline for that greater offense with respect to sentencing. USSG §1B1.2(a). Under the revised comment to USSG §1B1.2, however, the defendant must explicitly agree that a factual statement or stipulation will have that effect. This can be tricky, and defense attorneys must be aware of this predicament. A mistake here could mean the difference of decades in prison. For example, if that condition was met, and the defendant pled guilty to one offense, but stipulated to a more serious offense in the factual basis, the court would sentence the defendant based on the guideline for the more serious offense. So, if the defendant pled guilty to bank larceny, but stipulated to bank robbery, he is sentenced for bank robbery. With respect to appealing the factual basis, inadequacy of the factual basis is waived if at sentencing the defendant failed to raise the issue and the defense counsel agreed that a basis existed.

Sample Plea Agreement Language: The Defendant is pleading guilty because he is in fact guilty. The Defendant certifies that he does hereby admit that the facts set forth below are true, and were this case to go to trial, the United States would be able to prove those specific facts and others beyond a reasonable doubt.

————— • —————

CHAPTER 2

WARNINGS

———•———

The warnings are usually spread out within the plea agreement, often quite obviously. They have been grouped here for discussion with corresponding sample language.

SECTION 1

PERJURY AND OTHER FALSE STATEMENT OFFENSES

———•———

This paragraph makes explicit the policy set out in USSG §1B1.8(b)(3) regarding the use of information provided in cooperation agreements in a later perjury prosecution.

Sample Plea Agreement Language: Nothing in this agreement shall be construed to protect the defendant in any way from prosecution for perjury, false declaration or false statement, as defined by the law of any sovereign, or any other offense committed by the defendant after the date of this agreement. Any information, statements, documents, and evidence, which the defendant provides to the United States pursuant to this agreement, may be used against him in any such prosecutions.

SECTION 2

REINSTITUTION OF PROSECUTION

This is the government side of the "back to square one" provision. Because under some circumstances a defendant may be able to withdraw from a plea or have a plea set aside on appeal, the government wants to be able to get back to the status quo ante in that event. This kind of provision is not unfair; but, it is very hard to explain to poorly educated or non-English speaking clients.

Sample Plea Agreement Language: If the defendant's guilty plea is rejected, withdrawn, vacated, or reversed at any time, the United States will be free to prosecute the defendant for all charges of which it has knowledge, and any charges that have been dismissed because of this plea agreement will be automatically reinstated. In such event, the defendant waives any objections, motions, or defenses based upon the Statute of Limitations, the Speedy Trial Act or constitutional restrictions on bringing of charges.

SECTION 3

DISCLOSURE OF INFORMATION TO PROBATION OFFICE AND COURT

———— • ————

This provision describes, and perhaps causes, a problem: the probation office gets the information on all the conduct known to the prosecutor, even if the defendant only pleads to part of it. This is the genesis of the issues regarding consideration of dismissed and uncharged conduct, because it requires the prosecution to give the probation officer information on such conduct, which the officer then uses to increase the defendant's guidelines. I don't think I will ever agree with this practice. I'm not even sure if I was a prosecutor that I would agree with it. Regardless, it is important to note a similar provision in a plea agreement saying that the government was free to provide all relevant information to the court at sentencing was held to override the protected nature of statements made during a proffer in plea negotiations, even though the proffer agreement itself provided the information would not be used. In a case where that fact pattern arose, the judge at sentencing asked the government why the defendant was not entitled to a minimal role adjustment and the government used information from the proffers to show that the defendant had engaged in several drug deals. The court of appeals in that case held that the language in the plea agreement overrode the proffer agreement.

Sample Plea Agreement Language: The defendant understands the United States' obligation to provide all information in its file regarding the defendant, including charged and uncharged criminal offenses, to the United States Probation Office.

SECTION 4

EFFECT ON FORFEITURE AND CIVIL PROCEEDINGS

———— • ————

This provision reflects the government's concern that the Double Jeopardy Clause may be implicated when a defendant receives a sentence in one proceeding and suffers a civil forfeiture in another. Criminal forfeiture is an action brought as a part of the criminal prosecution of a defendant. It is an in-personam (against the person) action and requires that the government indict (charge) the property used or derived from the crime along with the defendant. If the jury finds the property forfeitable, the court issues an order of forfeiture.

For forfeitures pursuant to the Controlled Substances Act (CSA), Racketeer Influenced and Corrupt Organizations (RICO), as well as money laundering and obscenity statutes, there is an ancillary hearing for third parties to assert their interest in the property. Once the interests of third parties are addressed, the court issues a final forfeiture order. Civil judicial forfeiture is an in-rem (against the property) action brought in court against the property. The property is the defendant's and no criminal charge against the owner is necessary.

Administrative forfeiture is an in-rem action that permits the federal seizing agency to forfeit the property without judicial involvement. The authority for a seizing agency to start an administrative forfeiture action is found in the Tariff Act of 1930, 19 U.S.C. § 1607. Property that can be administratively forfeited is: merchandise the importation of which is prohibited, a conveyance used to import, transport, or store a controlled substance, a monetary instrument, or other property that does not exceed $500,000 in value.

Sample Plea Agreement Language: Nothing in this agreement shall be construed to protect the defendant from civil forfeiture proceedings or prohibit the United States from proceeding with and/or initiating an action for civil forfeiture. Further, this agreement does not preclude the United States from instituting any civil or administrative proceedings as may be appropriate now or in the future.

———•———

CHAPTER 3

COLLATERAL CONSEQUENCES OF PLEA

———— • ————

There are numerous collateral consequences to pleading guilty. Undoubtedly, there are a wide variety of collateral consequences to a criminal conviction. Although it appears to be common knowledge, the defense counsel would be well served to ensure that clients are educated on this issue, and there is no "common knowledge" defense to ineffective assistance of counsel claims. It may also be appropriate for the defense counsel to document in writing that the subject of collateral consequences has been discussed with the client(s) before a plea agreement is accepted. Both the American Bar Association and the U.S. Department of Justice have issued comprehensive reports on the subject of collateral consequences that are excellent resources for the defense counsel.

———— • ————

SECTION 1

LOSS OF RIGHT TO CARRY FIREARMS

A plea to a felony under federal law will preclude the defendant from bearing firearms under 18 U.S.C. §922(g) and §921(a)(20). There is no provision for restoration of this right for federal felons except for petitions to the Secretary of the Treasury under 18 U.S.C. §925(c), which are no longer being processed. A state cannot restore a federal felon's right to bear arms.

SECTION 2

IMMIGRATION CONSEQUENCES

The immigration consequences of a plea agreements are very complex and are beyond the scope of this book. Indeed, with ever-changing political policies, the immigration issues are likely to stay complex. Presently, nonresident aliens convicted of a felony are subject to deportation. Defense counsel should be aware that loss of status, deportation, and other immigration consequences may be even more severe than the criminal sanctions that gave rise to the deportation issues. Whenever the defendant has any kind of immigration status, the consequences of a plea on that status should be evaluated and explained to the defendant prior to the decision to plead. In some cases, pleas can be structured, agreements can be made, or at the very least arrangements can be made, so as to minimize the ill effect on the client.

SECTION 3

LOSS OF FEDERAL BENEFITS

The U.S. Department of Housing and Urban Development has a "zero tolerance" policy, under which any conviction involving drugs or violence is grounds for eviction from public housing. Persons convicted of drug-related felonies are subject to a lifetime ban on Temporary Assistance to Needy Families and food stamps. Similarly, a drug-related conviction disqualifies an individual from receiving federal education grants, loans and work assistance. Completion of a drug rehabilitation program can restore the person's eligibility.

SECTION 4

MILITARY SERVICE AND BENEFITS

———— • ————

Federal law prohibits felons from enlisting in any branch of the armed forces of the United States; however, the secretary of defense has the discretion to authorize exceptions. Persons convicted of mutiny, treason, sabotage, rendering assistance to the enemy or other specifically enumerated offenses are barred from receiving all forms of veteran's benefits, such as pension, disability, hospitalization and burial in a national cemetery.

SECTION 5

FEDERAL CONTRACT EXCLUSION

———— • ————

Many federal agencies have adopted regulations providing that persons convicted of felonies are excluded from participating in contracting opportunities. Of note, health care providers convicted of program-related fraud can be excluded from Medicare and Medicaid, and persons convicted of fraud or any Department of Defense contract are excluded from working on a defense contract for at least five years.

SECTION 6

FEDERAL EMPLOYMENT AND LICENSURE/SECURITY RESTRICTIONS

———•———

Federal law automatically excludes felons from serving or continuing to serve as a law enforcement officer, without exception. Persons wishing to serve as airport security screeners, or who need access to secure areas of an airport, must not have been convicted during the previous 10 years of a wide variety of felonies. Similar restrictions exist for persons whose employment requires Transportation Worker Identification Credentials. Merchant mariners also must not have been convicted of certain enumerated offenses, including federal "dangerous drug laws." Airman certificates can be revoked for certain convictions, particularly those involving drugs.

SECTION 7

INTERNATIONAL TRAVEL

———•———

Conviction of a federal felony drug offense results in passport revocation if the offense involved use of the passport or the crossing of an international border. Even after passport rights are restored, convicted felons contemplating overseas travel must not forget to verify their eligibility for a visa with the destination country.

CHAPTER 4

APPROVAL AND ACCEPTANCE OF THE PLEA

———— • ————

Ironclad is a term that comes to mind when considering the reason for the approval and acceptance Sections of a plea. This phrase by definition means "too strong to be doubted or questioned." By requiring signatures from the defense counsel and the defendant, along with in some cases a Section on each page for the defendant's initials, the Court first wants to ensure that the defense attorney has done his or her job, but most importantly, wants to guard against any future appellate issues arising from the defendant's plea.

SECTION 1

DEFENSE ATTORNEY APPROVAL

———— • ————

The defense attorney approval Section requires defense counsel's signature rather than the defendant's. The purpose is to lock defense counsel in to vouch for the plea, as well as alert the Court that counsel certifies that he or she has properly advised the defendant regarding this plea.

Sample Plea Agreement Language: I have discussed this case and the plea agreement with my client in detail and have advised the defendant in all matters within the scope of Fed.R.Crim.P. 11, the constitutional and other rights of an accused, the factual basis for and the nature of the offense to which the guilty plea will be entered, possible defenses, and the consequences of the guilty plea. No assurances, promises, or representations have been given to me or to the defendant by the United States, or by any of its representatives, which are not contained in this written agreement. I concur in the entry of the plea as indicated above and on the terms and conditions set forth in this agreement as in the best interests of my client. I agree to make a bona fide effort to ensure that the guilty plea is entered in accordance with all the requirements of Fed.R.Crim.P. 11.

Failure to properly advise the defendant of the elements of the offense, defenses, or penalties, resulting in a mistaken decision to plead guilty, has always been understood as possible ineffective assistance of counsel. Further, failure to properly advise the defendant on sentencing guidelines, resulting in a defendant's decision not to take a plea bargain, can also be ineffective assistance. Failure to warn a client of possible career offender status has also been held to be ineffective assistance. The remedy for such failures is not completely clear, but one suggestion is that where a defendant failed to accept a plea bargain because counsel did not advise him or her of the existence of an offer, then the remedy would be modification of the judgment consistent with the plea offer the defendant should have been advised of, or a new trial with resumption of the plea negotiation process. To be eligible for relief, the defendant has to demonstrate that he would have accepted the plea had it been communicated.

SECTION 2

GOVERNMENT APPROVAL

————— • —————

Approval from the Government is typically a given considering that, more often than not, they are the drafters of the plea documents. The document must be signed by the drafter, who is usually an Assistant United States Attorney of record for the case, as well as the Chief United States Attorney for the District in which the case originated. The government approval Section is usually nothing more than a signature block, has no real significance beyond making the government a party to the contract, and commonly states, "I have reviewed this matter and the plea agreement. I agree on behalf of the United States that the terms and conditions set forth are appropriate and are in the best interests of justice." With respect to sentencing and the government's approval, there is typically a Section within the plea agreement where the government acknowledges its part in the plea agreement, and does a good job insulating itself for those times when a Court ignores the parties sentencing recommendations and renders a harsher than anticipated sentence.

Sample Plea Agreement Language: The defendant further understands and acknowledges that any discussions between he or his attorney and the attorney or other agents for the government regarding any recommendations by the government are not binding on the Court and that, should any recommendations be rejected, the defendant will not be permitted to withdraw his plea. The government expressly reserves the right to support and defend any decision that the Court may make with regard to the defendant's sentence, whether or not such a decision is consistent with the government's recommendations contained herein.

SECTION 3

COURT ACCEPTANCE

———•———

Rule 11(e)(2) allows the court to delay acceptance of the plea agreement until after the presentence report in the case of a Rule 11(e)(1)(A) or (C) agreement, and the guidelines require the court to delay acceptance of the plea agreement until the presentence report has been considered in most cases. USSG §6B1.1(c). Under the Guidelines, the court's acceptance of the plea is contingent on the court's consideration of the presentence report. Acceptance usually takes place on the record at the sentencing hearing, rather than at the change of the plea hearing. Previously, some courts began to accept the plea agreement at the time of the plea hearing to prevent the defendant from withdrawing from the plea before sentencing. The law used to allow for either party to be entitled to modify its position and even withdraw from the bargain until the plea is tendered and the court accepts the bargain. Indeed, unless and until the trial judge approves a plea agreement and accepts a guilty plea, neither party was bound by the agreement.

This controversy was laid to rest when the Supreme Court held that once a plea is entered, a defendant may not withdraw his plea unless he shows a fair and just reason under Rule 32(e). The sequence of events is important. Rule 32 prohibits the court from reviewing the Pre Sentence Report (PSR) before the guilty plea is accepted, and thus the court may not consider it in deciding whether to accept the plea (absent consent of the defendant). The court must accept the plea, read the PSR, and then reject the plea agreement if it is not to the court's satisfaction. At that point it is up to the defendant to decide whether to withdraw the plea, as the court may not vacate the plea on its own motion.

Sample Plea Agreement Language: It is understood by the parties that the Court is neither a party to nor bound by this agreement. The Court may accept or reject the agreement, or defer a decision until it has had an opportunity to consider the presentence report prepared by the United States Probation Office. The Defendant understands and acknowledges that, although the parties are permitted to make recommendations and present arguments to the Court, the sentence will be determined solely by the Court, with the assistance of the United States Probation Office.

PART 4

WAIVERS

The constant assumption runs throughout the law that the natural and spontaneous evolutions of habit fix the limits of right and wrong.

~ Benjamin N. Cardozo (1870 –1938)

WAIVERS

The waiver Section of a plea agreement usually covers two distinct types of waivers: first, there is the set of non-negotiable waivers that must accompany any guilty plea, such as the waiver of the right to trial, right to cross-examine witnesses, and the right to testify on your own behalf, and second, there is the more negotiable set of waivers that the prosecution attempts to include in return for the plea bargain, such as the waiver of the right to appeal.

———— • ————

CHAPTER 1

WAIVER OF TRIAL AND OTHER CONSTITUTIONAL RIGHTS

———— • ————

The general waiver Sections of plea agreements vary from minimal to extensive. Plea agreements waive many of the rights attendant on trial. Some plea agreements go further and contain a waiver of sentencing rights, such as the right to seek a downward departure. Although such waivers have become common in immigration cases, they are also beginning to appear in other types of cases.

SECTION 1

APPEAL WAIVERS MUST BE KNOWING AND VOLUNTARY

———— • ————

A waiver must be knowing and voluntary. A waiver *is knowing* if the court advises the defendant of the waiver or if it is manifestly clear that the defendant understood the full significance of waiver. The waiver will be upheld if either (1) the district court specifically questioned the defendant about the waiver during the colloquy, or (2) the record clearly shows that the defendant understood the full significance of the waiver. On the other hand, a waiver was struck down where the colloquy indicated that the defendant did not really understand it even though it was in the written agreement.

Unless there is a manifestly clear indication in the record that the defendant understood the full significance of his appeal waiver, a lack of sufficient inquiry by the district court during the Rule 11 hearing would be error and would invalidate the appeal waiver. There is also a possibility of implicit waiver of a defendant's appeal rights as to certain issues. Courts have held in numerous cases that a defendant waives any objection that he fails to make in the district court.

Sample Plea Agreement Language: The defendant acknowledges that he is entering into this agreement and is pleading guilty freely and voluntarily without reliance upon any discussion between the attorney for the government and the defendant and his attorney, and without promise of benefit of any kind (other than the concessions contained within this agreement), and without threats, force, intimidation, or coercion of any kind. The defendant further acknowledges his understanding of the nature of the offense to which he is pleading guilty and the elements thereof, including the penalties provided by law, and the defendant's complete satisfaction with the representation and advice received from the defendant's undersigned counsel. This guilty plea is not the result of force, threats, assurances or promises other than the promises contained in this agreement. I am not under the influence of any drug, medication, liquor, or other intoxicant or depressant, which would impair my ability to fully understand the terms and conditions of this plea agreement.

SECTION 2

WAIVER OF TRIAL RIGHTS

While it may be obvious, it is still paramount that an attorney explain and discuss that a defendant's plea waives his or her trial rights. The defendant will not get the trial by a jury of peers as is so-often quoted from the Constitution; rather, a trial is being avoided purposefully and in exchange for the terms of the impending plea agreement.

Sample Plea Agreement Language: The defendant understands that he has the right to plead not guilty or to persist in that plea if it has already been made, and that the defendant has the right to be tried by a jury with the assistance of counsel, the right to confront and cross-examine the witnesses against him, the right against compulsory self-incrimination, and the right to compulsory process for the attendance of witnesses to testify in his defense. By pleading guilty, the defendant waives or gives up those rights and there will be no trial in this matter.

SECTION 3

WAIVER OF RIGHT TO APPEAL THE SENTENCE

———— • ————

Typically, waivers contained within a plea agreement are absolute and do not carry any exceptions. However, when it comes to a defendant waiving his or her right to appeal the eventual sentence of the Court, there are exceptions.

Sample Plea Agreement Language: The defendant agrees that this court has jurisdiction and authority to impose any sentence up to the statutory maximum and expressly waives the right to appeal his sentence on any ground, including the ground that the court erred in determining the applicable guidelines range pursuant to the United States Sentencing Guidelines, except the ground that the sentence:

(a) Exceeds the defendant's applicable guidelines range as determined by the court pursuant to the United States Sentencing Guidelines;

(b) Exceeds the statutory maximum penalty; or

(c) Violates the Eight Amendment to the Constitution; provided, however, that if the government exercises its right to appeal the sentence imposed, as authorized by 18 U.S.C. § 3742, and

(b) As authorized by the foregoing statute, may be appealed by the defendant who is then released from his waiver.

CHAPTER 2

SOME APPEAL WAIVERS
MAY BE INVALID

———— • ————

Remember, a plea is a contract, and typically speaking, two parties can contract to receive or perform just about any *legal* thing. As discussed above, many pleas will contain agreements by the defendant to waive certain constitutional and/or practical rights. And, just like many contracts, one or both of the parties to a plea will use their respective leverage to require waivers and concessions of certain rights that one may not otherwise comfortably waive but for the present circumstances of a criminal investigation.

SECTION 1

WAIVER OF COLLATERAL REVIEW

———— • ————

In addition to waiving direct appeal, the below provision purports to waive any kind of post-conviction relief such as writ of habeas corpus. This may create an ethical problem, as the attorney who is advising the client to enter into the guilty plea is probably the same attorney that the client would be calling ineffective in a post-conviction action.

Sample Plea Agreement Language: Further, the defendant hereby waives any right to raise, appeal, and/or file any post-conviction, such as a writ of habeas corpus, concerning any and all motions, defenses, hearings, probable cause determinations, and objections which the defendant has asserted or could assert to this prosecution or to the court's entry of judgment against the defendant and imposition of sentence upon the defendant consistent with this agreement.

Can that attorney ethically advise the client to waive the potential claim against the attorney? Some bar associations have issued advisory ethics opinions on this issue, but the situation remains unclear. In the wake of those opinions, some defenders have sought opinions on the same subject from their state bar committees. The same type of conflict analysis should apply to waiving the right to make ineffective assistance claims.

———— • ————

SECTION 2

WAIVER OF BRADY MATERIAL PRE-PLEA

The government can require a defendant to waive his or her *Brady* right to disclosure of impeachment evidence as a condition of a plea agreement. *Brady material* consists of exculpatory or impeaching information and evidence that is material to the guilt or innocence or to the punishment of a defendant. The term comes from the U.S. Supreme Court case, *Brady v. Maryland*, in which the Supreme Court ruled that suppression by the prosecution of evidence favorable to a defendant who has requested it violates due process. Following *Brady*, the prosecutor must disclose evidence or information that would prove the innocence of the defendant or would enable the defense to more effectively impeach the credibility of government witnesses. Evidence that would serve to reduce the defendant's sentence must also be disclosed by the prosecution.

For example, let's say a defendant refused to accept a Fast Track plea bargain under which the government would recommend downward departure under Sentencing Guidelines if he or she pleaded guilty, because it contained a waiver of the *Brady* rights to disclosure of impeachment evidence. Further, let's say the defendant ultimately entered a guilty plea without an agreement, then appealed, challenging the government's refusal to recommend, and the court's refusal to grant downward departure.

If the Supreme Court were faced with this case, it would treat it as an issue of the voluntariness of the plea and likely hold that (1) the Constitution does not require government to disclose impeachment information prior to entering plea agreements with the criminal defendant; and (2) plea agreements requiring the defendant to waive his right to receive information the government had regarding any "affirmative defense" he would raise at trial did not violate the Constitution. In this specific example, the Constitution does not require such information to be provided to the defendant prior to plea-bargaining primarily because the need for this information is more closely related to the fairness of a trial than to the voluntariness of the plea.

SECTION 3

JURISDICTIONAL CHALLENGES NOT WAIVED

A jurisdictional challenge based on a defective indictment is not waived by the waiver of the right to appeal in a plea agreement. Nor will a waiver prevent an appeal where the sentence imposed is not in accordance with the negotiated agreement. If the sentence is outside the agreed range, the waiver clause is void and the defendant can appeal all aspects of the sentence, even those that did not violate the plea agreement. On the other hand, where the sentence does not exceed an agreed cap, the waiver is effective even though the sentence exceeds the guidelines and is not adequately justified as a departure.

Waiver of appeal may be subject to certain exceptions such as claims of breach of the plea agreement, racial disparity in sentencing among co-defendants, or illegal sentence in excess of the statutory maximum. A waiver is generally enforceable if the language of the waiver encompasses the defendant's right to appeal on the grounds claimed on appeal. This is reasonable, but somewhat circular. Appeal may also be allowed where the violation of rights appealed from occurs after the waiver, as where a defendant was arguably denied counsel at sentencing after attorney withdrew.

SECTION 4

ENTIRETY CLAUSE

Rule 11(b), FRCrP, lays out a laundry list of things of which the court must advise the defendant, including information about penalties that could be imposed, the right to representation (at no cost if needed), the right to go to trial and attendant rights, the effect of a plea of guilty on those rights, and a warning about testifying under oath. The foregoing list is set forth in the Sample Plea Colloquy in Chapter 1.

Sample Plea Agreement Language: This plea agreement constitutes the entire agreement between the government and the defendant with respect to the aforementioned guilty plea and no other promises, agreements, or representations exist or have been made to the defendant or the defendant's attorney with regard to this guilty plea.

Case law identifies notice of three particular rights as constitutionally essential: the right to confront accusers, the right to a trial by jury, and the privilege against compulsory self-incrimination. The above catch-all provision covers those Rule 11 rights not covered elsewhere in a typical agreement. Some attorneys dislike the reference to their competency, but the defendant will often be asked that question by the judge in one form or another during the plea colloquy anyway.

———•———

CHAPTER 3

SAMPLE FULL PLEA FROM THE DEPARTMENT OF JUSTICE WEBSITE

————— • —————

Below is the unsigned plea agreement from the famous case of *The United States of America v. John Lindh*. This agreement is extremely complete and encompasses a large amount of what this book covers; it also includes some provisions not discussed in the book. For an explanation of those provisions and more, the reader (you) is encouraged to reach out to the author (me) to discuss this book, its contents, and any questions about the *Anatomy of the Federal Plea*.

John Phillip Walker Lindh is a U.S. citizen who was captured as an enemy combatant in November 2001. Lindh received training with al-Qaeda, a known terrorist organization. Lindh took part in the *Battle of Qala-i-Jangi*, a violent uprising of Taliban prisoners. On February 5, 2002, a federal grand jury indicted Lindh on ten charges:

- Conspiracy to murder US citizens or US nationals
- Two counts of providing material support and resources to terrorist organizations
- One count of supplying services to the Taliban

- Conspiracy to contribute services to Al Qaeda
- Contributing services to Al Qaeda
- Conspiracy to supply services to the Taliban
- Using and carrying firearms and destructive devices during crimes of violence

If convicted of these charges, Lindh could be sentenced to three life sentences and 90 additional years in prison. Lindh pleaded not guilty to all 10 charges.

During Pre-Trial proceedings, Lindh claimed he was tortured into providing a full confession. The court scheduled an evidence suppression hearing, at which Lindh would have been able to testify about the details of the torture to which he claimed he was subjected. The government faced the problem that a key piece of evidence—Lindh's confession— might be excluded from evidence as having been forced under duress.

Michael Chertoff, then-head of the Criminal Division of the U.S. Department of Justice, then directed the prosecutors to offer Lindh a plea bargain: Lindh could plead guilty to two charges: (1) supplying services to the Taliban and (2) carrying an explosive during the commission of a felony.

As part of any agreement, Lindh would have to consent to a gag order that would prevent him from making any public statements on the matter for the duration of his impending sentence, and Lindh would have to drop any claims that he had been mistreated or tortured by U.S. military personnel *i.e.* he would agree give up his First Amendment right to free speech. In return, all other charges would be dropped.

On July 15, 2002, he entered his plea of guilty to the two remaining charges in accordance with the foregoing terms. The judge asked Lindh to say, in his own words, what he was admitting to.

"I plead guilty. I provided my services as a soldier to the Taliban last year from about August to December. In the course of doing so, I carried a rifle and two grenades. I did so knowingly and willingly knowing that it was illegal."

On October 4, 2002, Judge T. S. Ellis, III formally imposed a sentence of 20 years without possibility of parole.

———•———

IN THE UNITED STATES DISTRICT COURT FOR THE

EASTERN DISTRICT OF VIRGINIA

Alexandria Division

UNITED STATES OF AMERICA,	))))))))	CRIMINAL NO. 02-37A
v.		
JOHN LINDH, Defendant.		

PLEA AGREEMENT

Paul J. McNulty, United States Attorney for the Eastern District of Virginia, and Randy I. Bellows, David N. Kelley, and John S. Davis, Assistant United States Attorneys, and the defendant, John Lindh, and the defendant's counsel, James J. Brosnahan, George C. Harris, Tony West, Raj Chatterjee, and William B. Cummings, pursuant to Rule 11(e) of the Federal Rules of Criminal Procedure, have entered into an agreement, the terms and conditions of which are as follows:

GENERAL PROVISIONS

1. The defendant, John Lindh, pursuant to Rule 11(e)(1)(A), agrees to plead guilty to Count Nine of the Indictment and to a Criminal Information filed herewith. Count Nine charges the defendant with supplying services to the Taliban, in violation of Title 50, United States Code,

Section 1705(b), Title 18, United States Code, Section 2, and Title 31, Code of Federal Regulations, Sections 545.204 and 545.206(a). The Criminal Information charges the defendant with carrying an explosive during the commission of a felony which may be prosecuted in a court of the United States, in violation of Title 18, United States Code, Section 844(h)(2). The maximum penalty for the violation of Count Nine is ten years' imprisonment; a fine of $250,000; three years of supervised release; and a $100 special assessment. The penalty for the offense charged in the Criminal Information is ten years' imprisonment, consecutive to any term of imprisonment imposed on Count Nine; a fine of $250,000; three years of supervised release; and a $100 special assessment. The defendant is aware that any term of supervised release is in addition to any prison term the defendant may receive, and that a violation of a term of supervised release could result in the defendant's being returned to prison for the full term of supervised release. The parties agree that if two terms of supervised release are imposed in this case, the terms are to be served concurrently. See 18 U.S.C. Section 3624(e).

2. The defendant agrees that pending sentencing in this matter he will not seek release from detention.

3. Before sentencing in this case, the defendant agrees to pay a mandatory special assessment of one hundred dollars ($100.00) per count of conviction. Restitution is not applicable in this case.

4. At sentencing in this case, the Government will move to dismiss Counts 1 through 8, and Count 10.

SENTENCING MATTERS

5. Pursuant to Rule 11(e)(1)(B), the parties stipulate and agree that the correct application of the United States Sentencing Guidelines is as follows:

i. As to Count Nine, the most analogous offense guideline is Section 2M5.2. The applicable base offense level is 26. A twelve-level upward adjustment is appropriate because the provisions of § 3A1.4 apply. The defendant's criminal history category, therefore, is Category VI. A three-level reduction is appropriate for Acceptance of Responsibility, pursuant to § 3E1.1(a) and (b), resulting in an Offense Level Total for Count Eight of 35. Accordingly, the Sentencing Guideline Range on Count Eight is 292-365 months, subject to the statutory maximum of ten years' imprisonment.

ii. As to the offense charged in the Criminal Information, the offense guideline is Section 2K2.4, and the guideline sentence is ten years' imprisonment.

iii. Accordingly, the appropriate total sentence of imprisonment is twenty years. Neither party will seek an upward or downward departure from that sentence.

iv. As to both Count Nine and the offense charged in the Criminal Information, no fine is appropriate.

6. The defendant is aware that 18 U.S.C. Section 3742 affords a defendant the right to appeal the sentence imposed. Acknowledging all this, the defendant knowingly waives the right to appeal any sentence up to and including

twenty years' imprisonment, or the manner in which that sentence was determined, on the grounds set forth in 18 U.S.C. Section 3742 or on any ground whatever, in exchange for the concessions made by the United States in this plea agreement. This agreement does not affect the rights or obligations of the United States to appeal as set forth in 18 U.S.C. Section 3742(b).

7. The United States will not further criminally prosecute the defendant for the specific conduct described in the Indictment, the Criminal Information, or the Statement of Facts.

WAIVER OF RIGHTS

8. The defendant represents to the Court that the defendant is satisfied that his attorneys have rendered effective assistance. The defendant understands that by entering into this agreement, the defendant surrenders certain rights as provided in this agreement. The defendant understands that the rights of criminal defendants include the following:

a. If the defendant persisted in a plea of not guilty to the charges, the defendant would have the right to a speedy jury trial with the assistance of counsel. The trial may be conducted by a judge sitting without a jury if the defendant, the United States, and the judge all agree.

b. If a jury trial is conducted, the jury would be composed of twelve laypersons selected at random. The defendant and the defendant's attorney would assist in selecting the jurors by removing prospective jurors for cause where actual bias or other disqualification is shown, or by removing prospective jurors without cause by exercising peremptory challenges. The jury would have to agree unanimously before it could return a verdict of either guilty or not guilty. The jury would be instructed that the defendant is presumed innocent, that it could not convict the defendant unless, after hearing all the evidence, it was persuaded of the defendant's guilt beyond a reasonable doubt, and that it was to consider each charge separately.

c. If a trial is held by the judge without a jury, the judge would find the facts and, after hearing all the evidence and considering each count separately, determine whether or not the evidence established the defendant's guilt beyond a reasonable doubt.

d. At a trial, the United States would be required to present its witnesses and other evidence against the defendant. The defendant would be able to confront those witnesses and the defendant's attorney would be able to cross-examine them. In turn, the defendant could present witnesses and other evidence in defendant's own behalf. If the witnesses for the defendant would not appear voluntarily, the defendant could require their attendance through the subpoena power of the Court.

e. At a trial, the defendant could rely on a privilege against self-incrimination to decline to testify, and no inference of guilt could be drawn from the refusal of the defendant to testify. If the defendant desired to do so, the defendant could testify in the defendant's own behalf.

TERMS OF COOPERATION

9. The defendant agrees to cooperate fully, truthfully and completely with the United States, and provide all information known to the defendant. A failure to cooperate fully, truthfully and completely is a breach of this plea agreement, as determined by the Court. The defendant acknowledges that he has been advised that the United States will not seek a downward departure from the applicable sentencing guidelines, or from the sentence imposed, pursuant to Section 5K of the Sentencing Guidelines, Title 18 U.S.C. Section 3553(e), or Rule 35(b) of the Federal Rules of Criminal Procedure, in respect to the defendant's cooperation. In regard to that cooperation:

a. The defendant agrees to testify fully, truthfully and completely at any grand juries, trials or other proceedings, including military tribunals.

b. As required by the United States, the defendant agrees to be available for debriefing by law enforcement and intelligence officers and for pre-trial conferences with prosecutive authorities. The timing and location of such debriefings and meetings shall be determined by the United States. Should defense counsel wish to attend particular debriefings, the Government will seek to schedule such debriefings consistent with the schedule of defendant's counsel, who shall make themselves reasonably available.

c. The defendant agrees to provide all documents, records, writings, or materials, objects or things of any kind in the defendant's possession or under the defendant's care, custody, or control relating directly or indirectly to all areas of inquiry and investigation, excepting documents privileged under the attorney-client privilege.

d. The defendant agrees that, upon request of the United States, the defendant will voluntarily submit to polygraph examinations to be conducted by a polygraph examiner of the United States' choice. The defendant stipulates to the admissibility of the results of this polygraph examination if later offered in a proceeding to determine the defendant's compliance with this plea agreement; however, the defendant reserves the right to challenge the weight that should be attributed to such polygraphs by contesting the accuracy of such polygraphs.

e. The defendant agrees that the accompanying Statement of Facts is limited to information to support the plea. The defendant will provide more detailed facts relating to this case during ensuing debriefings.

f. The defendant is hereby on notice that he may not violate any federal, state, or local criminal law while cooperating with the government.

ADDITIONAL GENERAL PROVISIONS

10. The United States agrees not to use any truthful information provided pursuant to this agreement against the defendant in any other criminal prosecution against the defendant. Regardless of any other provision of this agreement, however, the United States may use any statement made by the defendant, whether in the form of the Statement of Facts accompanying this plea agreement or in the debriefing of the defendant or in some other form, against the defendant in any prosecution of the defendant

resulting from the defendant's breach of the plea agreement, whether such breach is caused by the defendant's providing false information, failing to provide full and complete cooperation, or for any other valid reason. Such a prosecution includes, but is not limited to, a prosecution for perjury or false statements.

11. This plea agreement does not restrict the Court or Probation Office's access to information and records in the possession of the United States.

12. This plea agreement is not conditioned upon charges being brought against any other individual. This plea agreement is not conditioned upon any outcome in any pending investigation. This plea agreement is not conditioned upon any result in any future prosecution which may occur because of the defendant's cooperation. This plea agreement is not conditioned upon any result in any future grand jury presentation or trial involving charges resulting from this investigation. This plea agreement is conditioned upon the defendant's providing full, complete and truthful cooperation.

13. The accompanying Statement of Facts signed by the Defendant is hereby incorporated into this Plea Agreement. Defendant adopts the Statement of Facts and agrees that the facts therein are accurate in every respect and that had the matter proceeded to trial, the United States would have proved those facts beyond a reasonable doubt.

ASSIGNMENT OF ANY PROFITS OR PROCEEDS FROM PUBLICITY

14. The Defendant hereby assigns to the United States any profits or proceeds, which he may be entitled to receive in connection with any publication or dissemination of information relating to illegal conduct alleged in the Indictment. This assignment shall include all profits and proceeds for the benefit of the Defendant, regardless of whether such profits and proceeds are payable to himself or to others, directly or indirectly, for his benefit or for the benefit of the Defendant's associates or a current or future member of the Defendant's family. The Defendant shall not circumvent this assignment by assigning the rights to his story to an associate or to a current or future member of the Defendant's family, or to another person or entity who would provide some financial benefit to the Defendant, to the Defendant's associates, or to a current or future member of the Defendant's family. Moreover, the Defendant shall not circumvent this assignment by communicating with an associate or a family member for the purpose of assisting or facilitating their profiting from a public dissemination, whether or not such an associate or other family member is personally or directly involved in such dissemination.

SPECIAL ADMINISTRATIVE MEASURES

15. The Defendant is aware of the provisions of 28 C.F.R. Section 501.2 governing conditions of incarceration in national security cases. If a determination is made that such special administrative measures are applicable, the government will endeavor nonetheless to treat the Defendant in a manner comparable to the treatment of other

federal inmates at the same security classification level, regarding such matters as access to educational opportunities, prison library privileges, books, magazines, newspapers, radio and television, visitation, and religious observances. The government also will endeavor to modify the currently existing special administrative measures to effect the same result.

SUPERVISED RELEASE

16. During the period of supervised release, the Defendant may in appropriate circumstances apply to the Court and his probation officer for permission to travel out of his district of supervision, including out of the country. See U.S.S.G. Section 5D1.3(c)(1).

BREACH OF THE PLEA AGREEMENT

17. Any alleged breach of this agreement by either party shall be determined by the Court in an appropriate proceeding at which the Defendant's disclosures and documentary evidence shall be admissible and at which the moving party shall be required to establish a breach of the plea agreement by a preponderance of the evidence.

18. If the Defendant fails in any way to fulfill completely all of the obligations under this plea agreement, including but not limited to his candid, forthright, truthful and complete cooperation, the United States may seek release from any or all its obligations under this plea agreement. If released from its obligations under this plea agreement, the United States may prosecute the Defendant to the full extent of the law. The Defendant agrees that any prosecution and sentencing subsequent to a breach of this plea agreement is

not barred by the Double Jeopardy Clause of the Constitution or any other Constitutional provision or law or rule and that such rights as he might otherwise have enjoyed under these provisions are hereby waived, except that the Defendant may raise any defense or make any claim that he could have raised prior to the entry of the Plea Agreement.

19. If the Defendant fails to fulfill his obligations under this plea agreement, and the matter proceeds to trial, the Defendant understands and agrees that any statements he makes pursuant to or associated with this plea agreement, including but not limited to the Statement of Facts submitted in connection with this plea agreement and such statements as the Defendant makes during the debriefing process, are admissible if offered by the Government at pre-trial proceedings and/or at trial and may be used for any purpose. Defendant shall assert no claim under the United States Constitution, any statute, Rule 410 of the Federal Rules of Evidence, Rule 11(e)(6) of the Federal Rules of Criminal Procedure, or any other federal rule, that Defendant's statements pursuant to this agreement should be suppressed or are inadmissible, except on relevancy grounds.

DESIGNATION

20. The Government agrees not to object to the Defendant's request to the Court for a recommendation that he be assigned to a suitable Bureau of Prisons facility near his parents' homes. The Government further agrees to communicate to the Bureau of Prison, at the Defendant's request, factors potentially relevant to the secure

incarceration of the Defendant during his term of imprisonment, and to make appropriate recommendations as to those factors, including recommendations related to personal safety. The parties recognize that it is solely within the discretion of the Bureau of Prisons to determine where and in what manner the Defendant is actually incarcerated, and this plea agreement in no way limits the exercise of that discretion.

UNLAWFUL ENEMY COMBATANT STATUS

21. With the following exception, the United States agrees to forego any right it has to treat the Defendant as an unlawful enemy combatant based on the conduct alleged in the Indictment. The exception is as follows: For the rest of the defendant's natural life, should the Government determine that the Defendant has engaged in conduct proscribed by the offenses now listed at 18 U.S.C. § 2332b(g)(5)(B), or conduct now proscribed under 50 U.S.C. § 1705, the agreement contained in this paragraph shall be null and void, and the United States may immediately invoke any right it has at that time to capture and detain the Defendant as an unlawful enemy combatant based on the conduct alleged in the Indictment.

REPRESENTATIONS BY THE DEFENDANT

22. The Defendant agrees that this agreement puts to rest his claims of mistreatment by the United States military, and all claims of mistreatment are withdrawn. The Defendant acknowledges that the U.S. military did not intentionally mistreat him.

CREDIT FOR TIME SERVED

23. The United States recommends that the Defendant be given credit by the Bureau of Prisons for such time as he has been in custody of the United States, including the time period between December 1, 2001 and January 22, 2002, while the Defendant was in the custody of the United States military. The parties recognize and acknowledge that the Bureau of Prisons will determine the computation of credit for time served.

CONCLUDING REPRESENTATIONS

24. This written agreement constitutes the complete plea agreement between the United States, the Defendant, and the Defendant's counsel. The United States has made no promises or representations except as set forth in writing in this plea agreement.

25. The Defendant acknowledges that no threats have been made against the Defendant and that the Defendant is pleading guilty freely and voluntarily because the Defendant is guilty. Any modification of this plea agreement shall be valid only as set forth in writing in a supplemental or revised plea agreement signed by all parties.

26. Defendant's Signature: I hereby agree that I have consulted with my attorney and fully understand all rights with respect to the indictment. Further, I fully understand all rights with respect to the provisions of the Sentencing Guidelines and Policy Statements, which may apply in my case. I have read this plea agreement and carefully

reviewed every part of it with my attorney. I understand this agreement and I voluntarily agree to it.

_____
DEFENDANT

Date:_____

27. Defense Counsel Signature: We are counsel for the defendant in this case. We have fully explained to the Defendant the Defendant's rights with respect to the pending indictment. Further, we have reviewed the provisions of the Sentencing Guidelines and Policy Statements and we have fully explained to the Defendant the provisions of those Guidelines, which may apply in this case. We have carefully reviewed every part of this plea agreement with the Defendant.

To our knowledge, the Defendant's decision to enter into this agreement is an informed and voluntary one.

_____
DEFENSE ATTORNEY

Date:_____

Respectfully submitted,

UNITED STATES ATTORNEY

By:_____

Assistant United States Attorney

John G. DeGirolamo, Esq.

APPROVED:

_____

Date:

AUTHOR BIO

JOHN BEGAN HIS legal career during law school as a clerk for a trial practice, which concentrated in medical malpractice defense. Out of law school, John was hired to the litigation department of the semi-national firm Butler & Hosch. Having spent two years at the firm, it became clear to John that he missed the criminal law he spent his college and law school careers studying.

The law firm of Charles M. Greene, which carries a high-level practice of State and Federal criminal defense and complex commercial litigation, hired John after his two years at Butler & Hosch. Under the tutelage of the managing partner, Charles Greene, along with the other colleagues at the firm and co-counsel with which the firm works very closely, John was able to learn from attorneys that are considered the best of the best in the local and statewide communities.

For 2014 and 2015, Attorney John DeGirolamo was selected by The National Trial Lawyers of America as a *Top 40 under 40 in Florida*! Attorney John DeGirolamo practices in the State and Federal Courts of Florida. He has experience handling high-profile cases in both the criminal and civil areas of law. The focus of his practice is in the areas of criminal defense, business litigation, as well as family law matters.

THANK YOU!

———•———

... for reading *Plea For Mercy*. We trust you have enjoyed these rich possibilities for understanding the impact plea bargaining has both on our legal system and the citizens it is intended to protect....

Thank you in advance for taking the time to post a review for the book on Amazon; many readers will not take that step to purchase and read... until they know someone else has led the way.

If you enjoyed reading *Plea for Mercy* I would appreciate it if you would help others enjoy the book, too.

LEND IT. This book is lending enabled, so please feel free to share with a friend.

RECOMMEND IT. Please help other readers find the book by recommending it to readers' groups, discussion boards, Goodreads, etc.

REVIEW IT. Please tell others why you liked this book by reviewing it on the site where you purchased it, on your favorite book site, or your own blog.

http://amzn.to/1U1JGcs

EMAIL ME. I'd love to hear from you.

JohnD@inlawwetrust.com
STAY CONNECTED on Social Media.

Website:	http://inlawwetrust.com/
Facebook:	http://bit.ly/JohnDeGirolamoFacebook
Twitter:	https://twitter.com/@JDinlawwetrust

www.ingramcontent.com/pod-product-compliance
Lightning Source LLC
Chambersburg PA
CBHW060559210326
41519CB00014B/3517